Praise for *The Hidden School*

"With a masterful touch, Dan Millman's *The Hidden School* will transform how we navigate our way through the seemingly everyday events of life, inspiring us to discover their hidden magic, all the while igniting the mystical essence within ourselves."

—Michael Bernard Beckwith, author of *Spiritual Liberation*

"Dan Millman's conclusion to his Peaceful Warrior saga is a remarkable odyssey of life, death, and meaning—the fully realized completion of a unique spiritual adventure. What a privilege to travel this unforgettable journey with him. This epiphanous work will stay with you long after you've read it."

—Ed Spielman, creator of the landmark television series *Kung Fu*

"In this compelling story, Dan Millman takes us on a quest for the secret of eternal life. He moves easily between worlds, using external action-adventure as a metaphor for an internal spiritual quest, providing both entertainment and self-reflection. *The Hidden School* brings to mind the adventures of Carlos Castaneda and the mysterious quest in *The Da Vinci Code*. This is a page-turner, both entertaining and provocative. If you can only take one book to read on your next vacation, this is that book."

—Ron Boyer, award-winning author, poet, and screenwriter

"In *Way of the Peaceful Warrior*, Dan Millman established himself as a master of teaching through story. Now, in this exciting adventure, he reveals how deep learning can be found in unexpected places. The wisdom he shares will illuminate many lives."

—Don Miguel Ruiz, author of *The Four Agreements*

"Dan's new book, *The Hidden School*, reminds me of the magic and mystery of *Way of the Peaceful Warrior*. This suspenseful, often humorous adventure shows the way to our own light, our own music, and our own way home. When I experienced adrenal fatigue syndrome in Tahiti back in 1986, *Way of the Peaceful Warrior* literally saved my life. Keep on keepin' on, Dan. I'll always be there with and for you. Thank-Q, brother."

—Quincy Jones, Grammy award–winning musician, producer, actor, and humanitarian

"The conclusion to Dan Millman's life-changing Peaceful Warrior saga was well worth the wait. This riveting quest through many exotic locations reminds readers what it means to follow a spiritual path in the modern world. Millman's journey includes memorable characters and daunting challenges on the way to wisdom and inner peace. It's a book for anyone interested in life's bigger picture and deeper currents."

—William Bernhardt, bestselling author of *Challengers of the Dust*

"A brilliant sequel to a timeless classic. Well done. I highly recommend this treasure."

—Caroline Myss, author of *Anatomy of the Spirit* and *Sacred Contracts*

"Dan's new book is a must-read journey of transformation. Few other books so skillfully combine story and substance as this Peaceful Warrior adventure."

—Tony Robbins, #1 *New York Times* bestselling author, entrepreneur, and philanthropist

"*The Hidden School* is filled with beautiful lessons that challenge your ideas of reality and push you to live a more inspired life."

—Amy Smart, actress and activist

SELECTED BOOKS BY DAN MILLMAN

The Peaceful Warrior Saga

Way of the Peaceful Warrior

Sacred Journey of the Peaceful Warrior

The Journeys of Socrates

Core Teachings

Wisdom of the Peaceful Warrior

The Four Purposes of Life

No Ordinary Moments

The Life You Were Born to Live

The Laws of Spirit

Everyday Enlightenment

Writing Guidance

The Creative Compass

Training Guidance

Body Mind Mastery

Inspiration for Children

Secret of the Peaceful Warrior

Quest for the Crystal Castle

Further information

---

www.PeacefulWarrior.com

The HIDDEN SCHOOL

Return of the Peaceful Warrior

DAN MILLMAN

New York London Toronto Sydney New Delhi

North Star Way
An Imprint of Simon & Schuster, Inc.
1230 Avenue of the Americas
New York, NY 10020

This book is a work of fiction. Any references to historical events, real people, or real places are used fictitiously. Other names, characters, places, and events are products of the author's imagination, and any resemblance to actual events or places or persons, living or dead, is entirely coincidental.

First North Star Way hardcover edition June 2017

NORTH STAR WAY and colophon are trademarks of Simon & Schuster, Inc.

For information about special discounts for bulk purchases, please contact Simon & Schuster Special Sales at 1-866-506-1949 or business@simonandschuster.com.

The North Star Way Speakers Bureau can bring authors to your live event. For more information or to book an event, contact the North Star Way Speakers Bureau at 1-212-698-8888 or visit our website at www.thenorthstarway.com.

Interior design by Davina Mock-Maniscalco

Manufactured in the United States of America

10 9 8 7 6 5 4 3 2 1

Library of Congress Cataloging-in-Publication Data is available.

ISBN 978-1-5011-6967-0
ISBN 978-1-5011-6969-4 (ebook)

To all those striving to live
with a peaceful heart
and a warrior spirit.

No two persons
ever read the same book.
Edmund Wilson

CONTENTS

PROLOGUE

Tales and dreams are the shadow-truths
that will endure when mere facts
are dust and ashes, and forgot.

NEIL GAIMAN

In 1966, during my college years, I met a mysterious service station mechanic I called Socrates, described in *Way of the Peaceful Warrior.* During our time together, Soc spoke of a woman shaman in Hawaii with whom he'd studied many years before. He also told me about a book he'd lost in the desert, and a school hidden somewhere in Asia, but the details soon drifted into the recesses of my memory.

Later, when I graduated, my old mentor sent me away with the words "No more spoon-feeding, junior. Time to learn from your own experience." In the years that followed I married, fathered a child, coached gymnastics at

Stanford University, and then taught movement arts while on the faculty of Oberlin College.

Eight years had passed since I first wandered into Soc's all-night service station. To the casual eye, my life looked as good as it had during my college years as an elite athlete. But I was haunted by the feeling that I was missing something important—that *real* life was passing me by while I played pretend in the shallows of convention. Meanwhile, my wife and I had agreed to a formal separation.

Then I was awarded a worldwide travel grant from the college to research martial arts and mind-body disciplines. This opportunity reawakened those memories and the possibility that now I might find the people and places Socrates had mentioned years before. I could combine professional research with my personal quest.

This book, which narrates a journey across the world, opens just after my adventure in Hawaii (recounted in *Sacred Journey of the Peaceful Warrior*) and concludes just prior to the climactic ending of *Way of the Peaceful Warrior*.

Having completed the first leg of my travels in Hawaii, I'd now set my sights on Japan. That was before a chance discovery changed everything and proved the saying "Whenever you want to do something, you have to do something else first."

It all began on a rainy September morning. . . .

PART ONE

A Book in the Desert

Fight nonviolently for a better world,
but do not expect to find it easy;
you shall not walk on roses. . . .
Pilgrims of justice and peace
must expect the desert.

DOM HÉLDER CÂMARA

ONE

A shower of leaves in the gray dawn drew my gaze out the rain-spattered window of my motel room on the island of Oahu. Dark clouds matched my mood as I floated between heaven and earth, rootless, drifting through the in-between. My summer on Molokai with Mama Chia had raced by. Now I had a nine-month leave of absence before resuming my teaching duties.

Walking across the carpeted floor, clad only in my underwear, I stopped and glanced at my reflection in the bathroom mirror. *Have I changed?* I wondered. My muscular frame, a carryover from my college gymnastics days and recent labors on Molokai, looked the same. So did my tanned face, long jaw, and customary crew cut from the day before. Only the eyes gazing back at me seemed different. *Will I one day resemble my old mentor, Socrates?*

As soon as I'd arrived on Oahu a few days before, I'd called my seven-year-old daughter, who excitedly told me, "I'm going to travel like you, Daddy!" She and her mom were going to Texas to visit with relatives for a few months, maybe longer. Once again I dialed the number she'd given me, but no one answered. So I sat down and wrote her a note on the back of a picture postcard, punctuating it with Xs and Os, acutely aware of their inadequacy during my absence. I missed my daughter; the decision to travel all these months was not one I took lightly. I slipped the post-card into a leather-bound journal I'd purchased a few days before to record notes of my travels. I could mail the card later from the airport.

Now it was time to pack once again. I pulled my well-traveled knapsack from the closet and dumped my belongings onto the bed: two pairs of pants and T-shirts, underwear and socks, a light jacket, a collared sports shirt for special occasions. My running shoes rounded out the minimalist wardrobe.

I picked up the ten-inch bronze samurai statuette that I'd found off the coast of Molokai—a sign pointing me toward Japan, a long-sought destination where I might gain insight into Zen arts and *bushido*, the way of the warrior. I would also search for the hidden school that Socrates had challenged me to find. My flight to Japan was scheduled to depart the next day. As I repacked the knapsack, inserting my journal, the samurai, and then my clothes, I could still detect a faint scent of the rich red soil of the Hawaiian rain forest.

A few minutes later, realizing how easy it would be to forget the postcard I'd slid into my journal, I unzipped the pack and tugged at the journal, trying to extract it without dislodging all my neatly folded clothing. It wouldn't budge. Frustrated, I pulled harder. As the journal came loose, its clasp must have caught the lining; I heard and felt a rip in the pack's fabric. Reaching inside, I felt a slight bulge where the piece of lining had pulled away from the outer canvas shell. Then my hand found and drew out a thick envelope with a short message from Mama Chia written on the outside.

Socrates asked me to give you this letter when I thought you were ready.

Ready for what? I wondered, picturing my Hawaiian teacher's silver hair, open smile, and large body draped in a floral muumuu. Intrigued, I opened the envelope and began to read a letter from Socrates.

Dan, there's no cure for youth except time and perspective. When we first met, my words flew past you like leaves in the wind. You were willing to listen but not yet ready to hear. I sensed that you'd face frustration made more difficult by the belief that you were wiser than your peers.

Since Chia gave you this letter, you're probably looking to the East for answers. But if you go east as a seeker, begging alms of insight, you'll receive only a pittance. Go only when you can bring value to the table of wisdom. I'm not just waxing poetic here. First you need to find a book I lost in the desert decades ago.

This has got to be one of Soc's pranks, I thought, imagining his poker face, the twinkle in his eye. *Instead of going to Japan, he wants me to find a book in a desert? Which desert?* A sigh died in my throat as I read on.

I have a feeling that what I wrote in that journal may provide a bridge between death and rebirth, even a gateway to eternal life—insights you're going to need before this is over. I can't be sure of any of this, since its precise contents and location are veiled in my memory.

The story of its origins is tied to my personal history: I was born in Russia nearly a century ago and raised as a military cadet. Much later, on the warrior's path, I encountered a group of masters in the Pamir region in Central Asia: a Zen roshi, a Sufi, a Taoist, a master of the Kabbalah, a Christian nun. They offered insight and training in esoteric arts, but it would take me years to integrate what I'd learned. In my midforties, I immigrated to the United States near the end of the First World War. I attended night school and devoted myself to reading, writing, and speaking English as well as any American. Later I found work in construction, then in auto repair, for which I had an aptitude. I moved to Oklahoma, where my daughter taught school. After a decade there I returned to New York City.

Late one afternoon in my seventy-sixth year, while I was walking through what's now called Greenwich Village, I stopped under the awning of a familiar antiquarian bookshop, where a gust of wind urged me inside. As usual, a jingling bell announced my arrival before the sound died as if smothered by a blanket. The musty odor of a thousand volumes filled the air. I walked the narrow aisles, opening a few books whose covers creaked like arthritic joints. I wouldn't usually remember or relate such details, but what occurred that evening etched a vivid impression.

My eyes were drawn to the oldest woman I'd

ever seen, sitting at a small table. As I gazed at her, she placed her hand on what looked like a thin journal, the kind with a leather strap and a clasp that locks with a key. She paged through one of several books on the table, then picked up a pen as if to begin a notation. Instead, she turned and looked up at me.

She had young eyes for a face so lined, eyes shining below bushy brows, and skin like the leather of her journal. She could have been Hispanic, Native American, or maybe Asian. Her face seemed to change with the shifting patterns of light. I nodded and turned to go, only to hear her voice beckoning me. To my great surprise, she called me by a nickname from my boyhood—the same name you called me.

"Socrates."

"You seem to know me, yet I don't recognize—"

"Nada," she responded. "My name is Nada."

"Your name is Nothing?" I said.

Her smile revealed the few yellowed teeth she had left.

To borrow time while I struggled to recall a place or time we might have met, I asked her what she was writing.

She put her hand on my arm and said with a Spanish accent: "Time is precious. My work is nearly done." She wrote something on a scrap of paper and handed it to me. "Visit me tomorrow at this address. You'll know what to do." As she rose slowly to her feet, she added, "Come early. The door will be unlocked."

The next morning, just after dawn, I found the apartment house at the address she'd given me, climbed one flight of squeaking stairs, and knocked softly on a door at the end of a dim hallway. No answer. She'd said it would be unlocked. I turned the knob and entered.

At first I thought the small studio was abandoned—empty save for an old carpet and a few cushions—the garret of a Zen monk or Catholic nun. Then I heard music so soft it could have come from an adjoining room or from my own memory. Seeing the glow of a lamp from an alcove, I passed an open window and felt a chill breeze. I found her slumped over the desk, her head resting on her arms. Next to her lay the open book, her journal, and a key to the clasp. A pen had fallen from her ancient fingers. Her arm was cold and dry as parchment. Only a discarded husk remained.

As I reached out to stroke her thin hair, the morning sun illuminated her face, lending it an ethereal glow. That's when I recognized her.

I was thirty-five years old when I first met Nada. Her name was María then—a Christian mystic from Spain and one of my master teachers from the gathering in the Pamir. She had recognized me, nearly forty years later, in the bookstore. I'd failed to recall her, so she became Nada.

She'd known the end was coming. An envelope on the desk contained some money, enough to dispose of her remains, I guessed. On the front of the envelope she had scrawled three words: "Cremation. No relatives." That and a telephone number. I slipped the journal into my knapsack and the key into my pocket. After gazing back at her for a few moments and saying a silent farewell, I departed, leaving the door unlocked.

When I returned to my own small apartment, I felt as if I'd awakened from a dream, but the weight of her journal in my pack proved its reality. After using the hall phone to place a call to the mortuary, I sat down with the journal but I didn't open it. Not yet. I wouldn't treat it casually, like a dime-store novel. Despite my curiosity about what this mystic nun might have written, I'd wait to read it until after I scattered her ashes.

In the early evening a few days later, I retrieved the small urn holding all that remained of María, now Nada.

At dawn the next morning, I entered the lower end of Central Park, where I walked past Umpire Rock and meandered northward, passing familiar landmarks and lakes until I came to the Conservatory Garden, still closed for a few more hours. Climbing the fence, I found a quiet place to sit in a small cactus garden surrounded by thick foliage. As the rising sun shone on the desert plants, I scattered her ashes.

After a moment of silence, I took out her journal and unlocked the clasp. The leather-bound book fell open to an empty page. I turned to the next page. Also blank. I flipped through the pages. All empty.

My initial disappointment turned to amusement as I recalled María's humor those decades past, and I wondered if she'd smiled at this final, Zenlike gesture of an empty book.

When she'd said, "You'll know what to do," I

assumed she'd meant calling a crematorium and disposing of her ashes. And in telling me that her work was nearly done, she'd referred to a life well lived, now ended.

As I reached to close the journal, it fell open to the beginning, where I discovered handwriting hastily scrawled on the first page, under the date 11 March 1946—the night of her death. On that page I found two items written for me in her final moments: first was a story I'd come across before. This time, I read it carefully:

> A merchant in Baghdad sent his servant to the market. The servant returned, trembling in fear. "Master, I was jostled in the market. I turned around and saw Death. He made a threatening gesture toward me, and I fled. I beg your leave and a horse, so that I may ride to a place I know in Samarra, where I can hide."
>
> The master lent him a horse, and the servant fled.
>
> Later the merchant saw Death in the crowd and asked, "Why did you threaten my servant?"
>
> Death replied: "I didn't threaten your

> servant. I was only surprised to see him here in Baghdad, for I have an appointment with him tonight in the town of Samarra."

This story about the inevitability of death was understandable given Nada's age and apparent foreknowledge of her imminent demise. But why would she want to share it with me in her final moments? The answer came as I read the two final lines at the bottom of the page:

> Dear one: Only death's counsel can bring you back to life. The empty pages are for you to fill with your own heart's wisd . . .

The unfinished word marked her last breath. Now I truly understood her words "You'll know what to do." As her last request and final instruction, she'd bestowed on me both a blessing and a burden.

When I closed her journal and picked it up, it felt as if I were holding her in my arms, as if her soul had flown from her body into the book.

TWO

Surely Socrates didn't intend for me to go and find a nearly empty book in the desert! *I already have a blank book*, I thought, glancing at the journal that had torn the lining of my knapsack, leading to the discovery of his letter. My journal also had a clasp and key like the one he had described, and already looked as frayed as I felt at that moment. I took a deep breath before submerging again into his story:

> *My "own heart's wisdom," she had written. What did my heart understand? What had I learned that might be worth sharing? In asking me to fill the empty pages of this slim volume, Nada had given me a purpose beyond everyday living, but one that I had little hope of accomplishing. Could I write*

any words of significance? The idea filled me with doubt.

Sitting in that cactus garden with her journal on my lap, I couldn't even think about writing in it. Instead, the notion came to me that it was time for a change. I decided I would travel across the country, passing through the deserts of the Southwest, to live out the rest of my life on the West Coast of the United States. After I settled in California or perhaps in Oregon, I would think about putting pen to paper.

Over the next few days, I packed up my apartment, visited the bookstore, and wandered through the city one last time. But the landmarks that absorbed me were internal ones. Pages of memory turning one by one.

Which led me to think of you, Dan, and the challenges and doubts you too must have faced in trying to integrate and embody what I've revealed to you. I still wonder how much one person can do to help improve or illuminate the life of another. I know firsthand that mere knowledge doesn't take away the difficulties of life. But a deeper understanding and expanded perspective may help us face adversity with greater resilience and spirit. The task

I now place before you—finding the journal that I lost—will test how well our time together has served you.

This letter was unmistakably Soc's. He wrote it most likely only a few years past. So clearly he was still alive at that point and had retained his sharp mind. I felt as though I were meeting his younger self for the first time. *What moved him to share his inner life so freely?* I wondered. *Maybe the old guy misses me as much as I miss him.*

With that thought, I turned back to his letter:

To help you understand what the journal has to offer, and how I lost it, let me return to my story: A few days after leaving New York City, I reached Denver. From there, a few rides took me south toward the Sangre de Cristo Mountains and through Santa Fe, New Mexico. I stopped there for a few days before catching a ride into Albuquerque, where I planned to head west along Route 66.

An hour or so west of Albuquerque, my ride dropped me off near an Indian pueblo and pointed toward what he said was a school down the road.

When the truck's dust cloud cleared, I could make out a few scattered bumps on the horizon, which could have been a ghost town or a mirage. I walked in the direction the trucker had indicated, intending to fill my canteen before returning to the highway.

A few minutes later, after passing a large granite boulder and some small cacti adorned with magenta flowers—it's strange what images come to mind—I came to a one-room adobe schoolhouse. Children played in a dusty yard bordered by a well-tended garden.

As I used a hand pump to fill my canteen, a little girl approached me and introduced herself. She made quite a first impression, boldly announcing that she would one day teach at the school. I mention this girl because she may be important, because I would see her again. Her name may have been Emma.

I returned to the highway and caught another ride through a day and a night and into the next evening. In the quiet of the desert country, somewhere in the Mojave Desert of Arizona, or it could have been after I'd headed north into Nevada, I thought of Nada and her ashes in that cactus garden. I decided to camp for the night about fifty yards off the road.

Sometime in the night I awoke in the grip of an alternate reality, as if I'd ingested peyote or some other psychotropic plant. A flood of inspired ideas filled me, so I seized the journal and began writing by moonlight.

At the same time, my body temperature rose and a feverish state took hold, pushing aside my conscious mind so the fruits of a deeper mind poured out onto the pages. I couldn't keep up with the flood of ideas. I can't recall whether the sentences were fully formed or even made sense. As the fever overwhelmed me, I continued to write, no longer aware of the words themselves or of my surroundings. My head throbbed. I felt dizzy and confused. The desert had entered me, bringing burning heat, then chills. Samarra, I thought. This is Samarra.

I have only dreamlike impressions of what happened next: I recall wandering along the highway . . . writing . . . sleeping in a riverbed . . . writing . . . stumbling and falling . . . more writing . . . night and day. . . . One day passed, maybe two or three, flipping past like the pages of a book, of her journal. I remember climbing out of a truck, clinging to the pack that held the journal.

I may have spoken to one stranger, maybe others. About the journal and what I'd written—about eternal life.

At some point, perhaps fearing that someone might take it from me or that I might drop it in the desert, I must have found a safe place to deposit the journal, with the intention of coming back to retrieve it. I may have climbed a hill. Impressions of darkness and light. A tunnel. A high place. Beyond that, nothing.

The fever waxed and waned. Sometimes a darkness overshadowed me. Other times I experienced moments of clarity, rays of light. Once I came back to myself as I stumbled along a road in the desert. Yes, I think it was the Mojave. Arizona or Nevada, maybe near the border. I can't be sure. Someone picked me up, and then someone else. I must have stumbled to the other side of the highway, where I was taken south and then eastward, back toward Albuquerque.

I was so lost in my fever that I could only remember where I'd come from, not where I was going. I caught myself muttering aloud more than once, speaking with insects and animals amidst glowing landscapes, real or imagined. In this waking dream a local man appeared. Hispanic, I think. He poured water on my head.

Later I felt a cool cloth on my forehead, saw a white ceiling. I was in a clean bed. A young doctor told me that I had nearly died and that I was in a clinic or infirmary west of Albuquerque. Maybe near that school where I'd stopped for water.

I remained weak for some time, drifting in and out of consciousness. My dusty rucksack sat on a chair nearby with my personal items. I didn't realize until later that the journal was gone. I had a vague feeling that I'd hidden it, but no recollection at all of a location.

After I left the hospital, I thought about trying to find it so I could read what I'd written. As I headed west once again, I gazed out car and truck windows at the passing desert, struggling to recall where I might have hidden the book, searching for any familiar landmark, waiting for a cue or impulse to turn around, to go back.

Even after I settled in Berkeley, California, I waited patiently for a memory or impression to surface. But I couldn't re-create the time or place. Maybe I wasn't meant to. This letter is the most I've written about it since those days in the desert.

Even as I write, images appear: a dark place, a tunnel, the sun-darkened skin of a local man, white curtains, a child's voice.

I know I haven't given you much to go on, Dan. But remember this: Wherever you step, a path will appear.

"A path will appear?" I sputtered. "Come *on*, Socrates, there's got to be something more!" But if there had been more, he would have remembered it, shared it.

I thought back on the time we'd spent together. In the rare moments when Socrates had seemed distracted, had he been thinking about the journal or the words he couldn't remember writing?

So where does all this leave me? I wondered, flashing back to a moment in my own life, just before my motorcycle smashed into the fender of a Cadillac that had turned in front of me, shattering my leg as it sent me somersaulting to the concrete. I could still recall the thought: *This isn't happening*. I had that same feeling now. None of it made any sense. Socrates had no idea where the book was hidden. Yet he wanted me to find it. I turned to the end of his letter.

What I wrote in that journal may serve you well. Or the words may only reveal the ramblings of a feverish imagination. The journey is its own reward, Dan. But you may find this treasure worth the hunt. Let your inner light show the way.

Good journeys,
Socrates

As I folded his letter and slipped it back into the envelope, I thought of the last time I'd seen him in the flesh. He was sitting up in a hospital bed in Berkeley, looking well enough, if slightly pale, after a brush with death. He must have written the letter sometime in the weeks or months that followed, and sent it to Mama Chia for safekeeping.

I gazed outside as the Hawaiian sun broke through and turned leaves into emeralds, but my attention was darkly shrouded by questions: *Why has Socrates given me this task? Is it an initiation or test—his way of passing the torch? Or is he just too old to find it himself?* When we first met, he'd claimed to be ninety-six years old, and eight years had passed since then. Yet I could feel his presence and picture him wiping grease-stained hands on a rag or chopping vegetables for a soup or salad he would prepare for us late at night in that old service station office.

His letter pointed to Albuquerque and a nearby school and infirmary. But the Mojave Desert stretched across parts of Southern California, Arizona, and Nevada. "Only thousands of square miles to search," I muttered sarcastically, as if he were sitting across from me. "I can just fly into Albuquerque, retrace your steps by driving west to the Mojave, and then start digging."

Or, I thought, *I can stick with my plan and fly to Japan*. I had my ticket. I was nearly halfway there, and about three thousand miles away from the deserts of the Southwest, which lay in the *opposite* direction.

I knew I couldn't visit every small hospital in New Mexico trying to access decades-old private records. *What Soc's asking of me isn't just difficult. I've done difficult before. It's impossible!* I found myself pacing around my hotel room, conversing again with the air: "Sorry, Soc, not this time! I'm not going to spend months playing Don Quixote of the Dunes, looking under every rock in the Southwest. I can't do it. I won't!"

Yet I couldn't dismiss what he'd written—that without the journal I'd arrive in Japan empty-handed, "a seeker, begging alms of insight." And I'd never refused Soc before. Just then I recalled a favorite trilogy, *The Lord of the Rings*, where little Frodo prevails against all odds and reason. *But that story is fiction*, I reminded myself. *This is real life!*

Socrates had once told me, "When opportunity knocks, have your bags packed." My bags *were* packed—for Japan! Everything was arranged. What if I hadn't found his letter? What if it had stayed hidden in the lining of my backpack? Well, I *had* found the letter. With a deep sigh I slipped it into my empty journal, which I stuffed back into my knapsack.

Back and forth it went: I *wanted* to go to Japan. I *didn't want* to go hunt for a mysterious book in the desert. As Socrates once said, "It's better to do what you need to do than to not do it and have a good reason." Did I *need* to find this journal?

I decided to sleep on it. But before I slept, I reminded myself again to mail the postcard to my daughter when I arrived at Honolulu Airport—a place for departures, a place for decisions.

THREE

The whirling dervish of my mind must have settled its affairs during the night. The instant I awoke I knew that I must make the effort—I owed it to my old mentor, and maybe to myself. So, for better or worse, his letter would change my plans and maybe the course of my life. My open travel voucher allowed me to cancel my Japan trip and secure a flight to Albuquerque.

On my arrival, I rented an old Ford pickup from an off-brand agency with easy terms—a cash deposit, no roadside service, and good riddance. Then I found a surplus store, where I traded my worn-out sneakers for a pair of hiking boots. I also acquired a large duffel bag, a canteen, a broad-brimmed hat, a compass, a folding knife, a flashlight, and a light sleeping sack, plus a small folding pick and shovel, sunscreen, and a book about desert survival, which did little to enhance my confidence. After stuffing my purchases into the duffel, I tossed it into the front passenger seat. In the lingering heat of early evening, I found refuge in a nearby motel.

So it came to pass that in my twenty-eighth year, in early September of 1974, on a blistering day in Greater Albuquerque, I walked the streets of Old Town, seeking out locals who might recall nearby clinics or infirmaries from thirty years ago. After reviewing Soc's letter about the young girl he'd seen, I visited a few natural food markets and alternative bookstores to ask if the proprietors knew anyone named Emma, who'd be in her midthirties now and who might be a schoolteacher. I hoped that someone once drawn to Socrates might gravitate toward such places. I also asked if anyone could recall a man named Socrates who might have passed through town decades ago. I had little else to go on.

None of the clerks knew a local teacher named Emma or had heard of anyone named Socrates (other than the ancient Greek). Dead ends and empty pages, one after another. I spoke to this ethereal Emma in my mind, calling out to her through time and space, reaching into that place where we're all connected: *Where are you?*

Later that afternoon, in a small record store, a fashionably dressed older woman overheard me and said, "Excuse me, but are you sure her name is Emma? I once met someone named Ama who taught elementary school outside of town."

I found a small school on the west side of town with a sign taped to the door: CLOSED FOR SUMMER. When I knocked, a receptionist appeared. She told me, "A woman named Ama taught here for one term, but she moved on. I think maybe she got a job teaching at one of those pueblo schools to the west, off Route 66."

When I thanked her and turned to go, she was already picking up the telephone on her desk. *Busy lady,* I thought.

I must have taken a wrong turn, because instead of finding a school I arrived at an adobe hut I'd passed once before. As I neared the entrance, I saw a hand-painted sign: SOUVENIRS. Indian blankets hung under a makeshift eave providing shade, beneath which rested various kinds of pottery and desert artifacts. In one bin I saw pieces of amber, each with a scorpion or another unfortunate creature frozen inside. I shivered as I glanced at the other specimens—a tarantula, a wolf spider, and the reclusive and deadly fiddleback spider. Each insect or reptile had a label: BARK SCORPION, WHIP SCORPION, CENTIPEDE. On a shelf nearby, a stuffed Gila monster kept vigil. In another case I saw a well-preserved diamondback rattlesnake, a sidewinder, and the Mojave green, a particularly venomous snake—all denizens of the desert that made me wonder again what I was doing here.

I jumped as a voice behind me said, "*Buenos días*. What can I do for you?" It was Soc's voice I heard, but when I turned, I saw quite a different old man, with the bronzed skin of Indian or Mexican ancestry. He sat amidst his treasures, gazing out into the dusty air and stringing beads onto threads that edged a colorful blanket. He looked as dry as the desert, reminding me of the ancient nun Socrates had described in his letter.

"Uh, yes . . . well, I'm looking for a woman named Ama. I believe she's a teacher."

The old man gave no sign that he'd understood. He only picked up another bead with slow, graceful fingers.

Struggling to recall my high school Spanish, I asked haltingly: "*¿Señor, sabe usted . . . ah, dónde está . . . una escuela pequeña . . . y una señora, uh . . . con nombre Ama?*"

His eyes brightened and he sat up straight. "*Ah, la señora Ama. Sí, una mujer muy fuerte, muy guapa.*"

Of course he knows her, I thought, shaking my head at this strange coincidence. A ray of hope. "*¿Dónde está . . . ?*" My tongue tripped over the words.

"*Mi hermano,*" he interrupted, "since you swim in Spanish like my uncle Brigante, who drowned in a river many years ago, it might be best if we speak in English."

"Uh, yes." I grinned back at him. "That would be easier." Reaching out to shake his hand, I introduced myself.

Making no move to take my hand, he said, "At first I took you for Greek."

"Why do you say that?"

"When you spoke, a Greek name came to mind."

"What name?"

He paused for a long moment before answering. "Do you like riddles? I quite enjoy them myself. I have asked and answered many riddles, so let me return the question. Name a Greek in your mind, and you'll know the Greek in mine."

As I looked up, I saw through the hut and out a window in back: the outskirts of Albuquerque lay just a few hundred yards away, obscured by the desert haze. Had I stumbled into Wonderland? "Well, Plato is a fine Greek name."

"A teacher of merit," he responded, still staring out into the desert. "But to understand a teacher, you must know the teacher's teacher."

This old *indio*, who spoke perfect English despite some missing teeth, was playing with me. He knew very well who Plato's teacher was, and he knew that I knew. "Plato's teacher was Socrates," I said.

"Some people call me Papa Joe, but since you've solved the riddle of the Greek, you may call me *abuelo* and I will call you *nieto*—grandson." Staring past me, he held his hand out in my general direction.

Before shaking his hand, I passed my own back and forth in front of his eyes and solved another riddle. "Ah, yes," he said. "*Ciego como un murciélago, listo como un zorro.*" Then he translated: "Blind as a bat, smart as a fox," He winked a sightless eye and added, "Many who see with their eyes are still blind. I have no sight, yet I see many things."

"What do you see?" I asked.

"I see into the place where riddles are born."

"And what do you find there?"

"That's a riddle for you to solve. But I will tell you this: My eyesight took flight in childhood. It turned inward, and has been soaring ever since. And how is *your* sight, *nieto*? Do you have eyes to find what you seek?"

This was getting weird, even for me. We were strangers to each other. All I had done was ask him about the woman.

"Okay, Papa Joe—*abuelo*. Why don't we just lay our cards on the table?"

"You like poker?" he asked obliquely.

"This isn't about poker. It's about life."

"Are they not the same?" he asked, in a voice like that of old Master Po from the TV show *Kung Fu*.

Losing my patience, I asked him directly, "Socrates, you knew him, right? Can you help me find a woman named Ama?"

"*¿Por qué?* Why do you seek this woman?" he asked, and his fingers returned to the beads.

"I think you know."

He remained silent, so I continued: "She may have met my friend, my mentor. I'm hoping she can help me find . . . something."

"Ah, looking for a *something*," he said with a knowing look. "Well, that may be difficult. There are many *somethings* in the desert."

"How do you know that it's in the desert?" I asked.

"I can't see. And yet I see. Do you see what I mean?"

"You really do like riddles, don't you?"

"Don't I?" he answered with another gap-toothed grin.

"*Abuelo*, please. I know you find this amusing, but I have to talk with this woman, Ama, and then—"

"I appreciate your passion," he interrupted. "You have a sense of mission. I only have a sense of humor. After nine decades of life, the concerns of youth—what other people think, finding love, achieving success—no longer concern me. What matters to me is amusement. That and what little I know about . . . *somethings*." He strung the last bead and knotted the thread.

Having completed his task, Papa Joe said, "There may be something I can tell you about *la mujer,* Ama."

"That would be helpful—"

"But first, I offer you a riddle."

"Now really isn't the best time for a game, *abuelo*."

"Life is a game," he said, "and now is always the best time. When you have no time for games, you have no time for life. You need to solve one sort of riddle. So indulge an old man in another. If you can do this, perhaps I can help you find this woman." As he spoke, he untied the knot and began pulling the beads from the thread.

"What if I *promise* to come back right after?"

"Ah, but we don't know what you'll find, or whether you'll return, or whether my soul will take flight in the meantime."

"I understand. But can you understand how pressed I'm feeling?"

"It's good to hear that you have feelings, *nieto*. That's how you know you're alive and that you care about something. But feelings must not run your life or mine. I no longer care for the dramas of this world. I've seen them played out in many forms. Now I await my death when I shall see once again as I do in my dreams."

"You believe that?"

"Perhaps not, but *¿quién sabe?* In the meantime, each new day brings another chance to learn and to serve some small purpose. Maybe I can help with yours."

I looked at the beads, now scattered around the naked thread.

"All right," I said, resigned. "Tell me your riddle."

"It's this," he said, leaning forward: "What is greater than God and worse than the devil? The rich want it, the poor have it, and if you eat it, you die?"

"What?" I asked.

Papa Joe repeated the riddle.

"I . . . really don't know," I answered.

"You're not supposed to know. That's why it's called a riddle," he said.

I turned my mind to it: *Greater than God. But also worse than the devil. Is it a play on words?* "Water?" I said. "Is it water, *abuelo*? I mean, Gandhi once said, 'To a starving man, God is bread.' So to someone in the desert, water may seem greater than God. Or if someone is drowning, water can seem worse than the devil."

"Nice try," he replied. "But no." He returned to stringing the beads.

"Well, then I'd guess—"

"Don't guess!" he said. "Wait until you know."

Frustrated by this waste of time, I ran the riddle through my mind, concentrating, looking at it from different angles. Nothing came to me. Meanwhile, Papa Joe picked up one bead after the next until the thread was complete. "I give up," I said. "Anyway, I can't take any more time for—"

"You have all the time you need until your time runs out," he said.

"Okay," I said with finality. "I've reflected, contemplated, cogitated, and ruminated. And I've come up with *nothing*."

"So!" he said, as his hand moved away from the knot he'd just tied. "You're smarter than you look," he added with a note of irony. "Nothing—*nada*—is the correct answer."

It took a moment before I got it. "Of course! Nothing is greater than God; nothing is worse than the devil; the rich want nothing; the poor have nothing; and if you eat nothing, you die."

Papa Joe was indeed as crafty as a fox—because there might be another layer to the riddle. So I had to ask: "*Abuelo*, did you ever meet a woman named Nada?"

He tilted his head, as if listening for something from his past. He smiled. "I've known many women by many names."

I waited. After a pause, during which I could only imagine him recollecting some of these women, he finally gave me detailed directions.

FOUR

An hour later, after following Papa Joe's directions in the sweltering heat, I found myself back at his souvenir store.

"I don't get it," I said, wiping my brow. "I did exactly as you said and wound up where I started!"

"Naturally," he explained, turning to face me, "I didn't want to waste my time telling you how to find the school until I knew you could follow directions." At this, he broke into such enthusiastic laughter that he nearly fell off his chair. After he'd regained his composure, he said, "Like I told you, *nieto*—all I have left are amusements."

I took a slow, deep breath. "Now that I've demonstrated my navigational abilities, would you be willing to direct me to the school where Ama may or may not teach?"

"Of course," he said. Pointing to the west, he said, "Go

down the road. Get off near the Acoma Pueblo. Seek the children who laugh and play, and you'll find Ama on that day."

"Thank you," I said, calming down. "I look forward to seeing children play. I have a child of my own—a little girl."

Hearing this, he brightened. "*¡Un momento!*" He rose from his chair and entered the shop. Finally he emerged and held out a leather-cloaked kachina doll painted red and green. "For *su hija*," he said. "I call her Standing Woman. Take good care of her. Such kachinas may bring help in times of need."

"Thanks again, *abuelo*," I said, tucking the doll into a side pocket of my pack.

Settling back into his chair, he dismissed my thanks with a wave and the customary "*De nada.*"

"Maybe I'll see you again."

"It's possible, but it isn't likely that I'll see you," he said, amused as ever by his own wit.

Papa Joe and his shop soon shrank, then disappeared from the rearview mirror. If he'd ever known the old sage Nada, he wouldn't say. But I finally knew where I might find the woman named Ama.

As the truck bumped along a dusty road just off the highway, I made a mental note to buy and send another postcard to my daughter. But how would I explain my presence in the Southwest when I couldn't even explain it to myself?

A few minutes later, I caught sight of a hand-painted sign that read ACOMA PUEBLO. At the bottom in smaller letters: ELEMENTARY SCHOOL.

I parked at the edge of the dusty schoolyard and made my way to the door. A few of the young children glanced my way, smiling and whispering to one another. Their teacher stood by an old desk. A handmade nameplate read "Ama Chávez." The stern-faced, bespectacled teacher, younger-looking than I'd expected, said in a strident voice, "Eyes front!" She nodded to me briefly, then turned back to an old blackboard with chalk that screeched as she wrote. Meanwhile, several children—first- and second-graders, I guessed—glanced back and made me a coconspirator in their fun.

When the school day ended, before I had a chance to speak with the teacher, a little girl ran up to me. She was, I guessed, seven years old—my daughter's age. She wore her hair in a ponytail decorated with a bright yellow ribbon tied in a bow, which reminded me of an embarrassing time when I'd dozed off while spying on Socrates only to discover that he'd fastened a similar ribbon to my hair as I slept.

The girl's voice brought me back to the present. "My name is Bonita and it means pretty in Spanish I am pretty don't you think?" she said without a pause. And after a big breath: "Bonita doesn't mean anything at all in the Hopi language but that's okay because I'm not Hopi I'm only part Hopi and part Mexican. Samatri my best friend who I'm mad at today says that since I'm only part Hopi then I'm only part pretty even if my name is Bonita. What's your name?" In a ladylike gesture, she slowly extended her hand.

"My name is Dan, and, yes, you're very *bonita*," I replied, taking her hand delicately. I took my own big breath, which made her giggle and take back her hand to cover her mouth. "Do you call your teacher Ama or Señora Chávez?" I asked, pointing to the woman erasing the board.

Imitating my style of speech, Bonita whispered to me as the teacher approached, "She's only the assistant and Señora Chávez will be back soon I heard because she had an errand. I think there's going to be a surprise party but it's not a surprise at all." She took a big breath. "Did you know that it's my birthday and Blanca's on the same day today?"

"No, I didn't know. I don't know a lot of things."

"You'll like Señora Chávez. She knows everything," Bonita declared.

About an hour later, just after kicking up to a handstand on the teacher's desk, I saw an upside-down woman enter the room carrying two bags of groceries. Even from my inverted position, I could see she was attractive. More important, she was real—and here! I quickly returned to my feet. Feeling like a student who'd been caught in some mischief, I introduced myself and started to offer an explanation.

She waved that away and said, "Bonita told me you were looking for me. You can explain your antics while I set up party decorations."

"I hear it's a double birthday."

"Bonita gets around," she said. "A future television host. Or first lady."

"Already a first lady," I said, reaching out for one of the bags. She hesitated, her body language sending a clear message: *Hands off, stranger.* But, changing her mind, she passed me a bag, then crossed toward an alcove with a small sink.

I placed the bag on the counter and said, "Ms. Chávez, I'm hoping you might be able to help me find something I've been looking for."

"Could you be more specific?"

"Would you like me to diagram a sentence?"

I thought I saw a faint smile before she turned away to lift a cake and party decorations out of the bag. "I'm sorry, Mr. Millman," she said, "I'm so used to being a teacher, I forget how to speak with surprise guests who drop by to help with children's parties."

She had a point. So I came to the point myself. As I taped blue and orange crepe paper to the wall, I said, "I have a mentor named after an ancient Greek. . . ."

I felt her eyes on the back of my neck. Yes, I had her attention. So I told her about the letter, about asking around Old Town and meeting Papa Joe. "He asked me to call him *abuelo* because—"

"Because he's older than dirt," she said, finishing my sentence. "I know him. And I may have once met your mentor." She turned and looked right at me, which is when I noticed that she had one blue eye and one brown eye—it worked for her. "I'd like to see this letter," she said. "This letter from Socrates."

FIVE

Seeing my reluctance, Ama added, "I don't need to read it. I just need to see it."

I reached into my pack, took the letter out, unfolded it carefully, and showed her the first page, then the last. She sighed. I have to say it was a lovely sigh. So I had to ask: "Do you and your husband live nearby?"

She looked at me knowingly. "I never married. But I do have a friend. Joe Stalking Wolf."

"You have a friend named Stalking Wolf?"

"A good friend. He's reservation police."

So much for my fantasies, I thought. *Joe Stalking Wolf* . . . Quickly abandoning that track of thought, I refocused on the matter at hand.

"In his letter, Socrates made a point of describing a bright little girl he'd met at a school."

"I was a spirited child," she said, smiling. "Or at least my father said so. And I didn't just meet Socrates at the school. I also saw him at a small hospital—a clinic and infirmary—while he was recovering from a bad fever."

"But why were you there?"

"My father was the primary doctor. He'd served as a medic in the military and worked in hospitals after that, one near Santa Fe and then in the clinic a few miles from here. Anyway, it was Papa Joe who'd stumbled over Socrates and brought him into the clinic."

"Papa Joe never told me. . . . How do you even remember all this?"

"Socrates had a way of making an impression, even on a six-year-old girl. He held my hand and told me I had an energy, a gift for healing," she said. "He had a beat-up old rucksack like some vagabond. I remember seeing it on a chair in the hospital. He muttered in his sleep about it, and about a book or journal. My father thought these were just feverish ramblings. Most days I went to the infirmary after school to wait. It's funny," she said. "Until you showed up, I hadn't thought about all this for a long while."

"Is it possible that Papa Joe visited Socrates in the infirmary?" I asked.

"I have a vague memory of seeing the two of them together. Maybe he came by to check up on the man he'd brought in. They seemed on friendly terms. That's it."

In the pause that followed, I resumed my decorating duties as Ama set out the cake and napkins. "You can be our special party guest," she said, and this time she meant it. "Would you call the children in for the party?"

When I stepped out the door, I saw a couple of boys climbing the lower branches of a great oak to a makeshift tree house. A few other children were playing on an old swing set. Meanwhile, Bonita and two other girls were watching a younger boy attempt to do a cartwheel. When I walked over to him and demonstrated the proper form, I was immediately surrounded by all the other children. So I showed them how to do cartwheels, out on that thin patch of lawn by the oak, in the late-afternoon sun.

A few minutes later, I heard Ama's voice. "Okay, everyone!" she called out. "Cake and ice—" The kids shot past me and ran toward their teacher.

"I think I had them at *cake*," she said as I followed her into the classroom.

When the party ended, and Bonita and the other children went home, Ama and I sat outside on an old porch swing, hanging from a tree branch.

"Multipurpose oak," I said, pointing up into the branches.

"It's their second classroom," she said. "Joe helped repair it. There's not much in the school budget for tree houses and repurposed porch swings." She laughed. "It was nice of you to teach the children cartwheels. They'll remember you." The softness in her voice told me, *You just made my A-list, and I wouldn't mind if you kissed me.* (At least, that's how it played out in my overactive imagination.)

"So just where *is* Joe Stalking Wolf these—"

She asked at the same time: "How did you come to have Socrates as a mentor?"

Resigning myself to this change of subject, I shrugged. "Lucky twist of fate, I guess. I'm glad you met him too, years before I did."

"We only exchanged a few words," she responded, "and for much of that he wasn't in his right mind."

"Then he hasn't changed much," I joked.

Ignoring my attempt at wit, she said, "You know, he told me some things that changed the way I see the world. I'd love to know more about him."

So, as the old swing swayed gently in the cool evening breeze, I shared a few highlights of my early days with Socrates. Her curiosity planted the seed of an idea in my mind: someday I might write about my time with Socrates and what I'd learned—when I finally understood what it was I'd learned. *Where would I even begin?*

I got up and retrieved Soc's letter from my knapsack.

Returning to the swing, I held it out. "Go ahead, read it. I think he'd approve."

As Ama turned the pages, I leaned back in the old swing. It was the first moment since I'd left Hawaii that I felt completely relaxed.

As Ama finished reading, a single star appeared in the northern sky. She looked up, her eyes open wide. "Until now, I never knew whether the journal really existed. He spoke of it, but it sounded like something from a dream."

"Did Socrates say anything about where he might have left the journal? Anything more about what he might have written in it?"

She looked toward the darkening horizon as though she might find an answer there. Turning back to me, she stood. "I'm sorry, Dan! I wish I could tell you more. I've enjoyed your visit. I have few friends with whom I can talk about such things."

"Other than Stalking Wolf," I said.

She smiled. "Yes, I can talk with Joe."

Dusk arrived. Class dismissed. We shook hands. Which turned into a brief, awkward hug. "Well," she said, "I have some class preparation to do. . . ."

I had preparations to do as well—homework assigned by my own teacher.

SIX

I walked out into the darkening desert scrubland. The light from Ama's classroom revealed an arid landscape that glowed faintly under a half-moon. I heard the hoot of a distant owl, the scuttle of a nearby lizard, and the chirping of crickets, shrill in the windless air. Out here and alone, I felt shadows of doubt that matched the darkening skies; the hairs on the back of my neck stood up. I turned to see the figure of a man ooze out of the shadows. As he drew near, my face broke into a smile.

"Abuelo!" I cried, seeing his gap-toothed grin. "What are you—?"

"*¡Silencio!*" he said, putting his finger to his lips. "You want to wake the desert?"

"It's already up."

"It must be, with you clomping around! I thought a

band of delinquents had come to do mischief," he said, taking an exaggerated martial arts stance. Then, more seriously, Papa Joe put a finger over his mouth. "There may be other creatures whose attention you don't want to attract."

I dismissed his antics as a flair for the dramatic until he said quietly, with a casual wave of his hand, "What if there were another man also looking for a *something*?"

Despite the warm evening, I felt a chill on the back of my neck. I looked around but saw only sagebrush and the dark horizon. *Another riddle?* I wondered. *What does he know?*

"If there were such a man, do you think that he might be deranged or dangerous?"

"Perhaps," Papa Joe replied, "but I no longer fear death, *nieto*—I wait for it. Death stalks us all, and is very patient. . . ."

The sound of his voice faded for a moment as I thought again about the story of Samarra.

"Anyway, I've seen my death, and it's not by such a man's hand. If he exists at all," the old man concluded.

I leaned against the wall, perplexed. *Why would anyone else be seeking the journal after all these years?* I thought. *Unless my asking around in Old Town . . .*

"How did you find me?" I asked in a whisper.

"Not important. What matters is that I'm here."

"But why? Is it because you have something more to tell me about Socrates?"

"Maybe yes, maybe no. That depends on you."

Resigned, I sighed. "Okay. Let's hear it."

He began: "Information can be as valuable as a precious gem. But is the information true? Is the gem real? How can you tell? Let's say you're given three sacks, each containing twenty identical gems. One of the three sacks is filled with impostors. The only clue you have is that the real gems weigh exactly one ounce each, while each fake gem weighs one-tenth of an ounce more. You have a scale. Not a balance scale with two trays—that would be too easy. Your scale has a single tray. In only *one* weighing, how do you discover which of the three sacks holds the impostors?"

"Wait—that's not a riddle, it's a math problem!" (Math was never my strong suit.)

Papa Joe said nothing.

I closed my eyes and pictured three sacks. I imagined what my cousin Dave, a math teacher, would say. *If I took one gem from each sack*, I reasoned, *those three gems would weigh a total of 3.1 ounces, since one of the gems would weigh an extra tenth of an ounce—one gem from each sack wouldn't reveal anything useful, but . . . what if I took a different number—?*

"Okay," I said slowly, following this thread. "I'd take

one gem from sack one, two gems from sack two, and three gems from sack three. The number of tenths of an ounce—either one-, two-, or three-tenths over six ounces—tells whether sack one, two, or three has the counterfeits."

"*¡Exactamente!*" he said.

Now I returned to my purpose. "I understand that you helped Socrates three decades ago, and that he may have told you about something he'd written in a journal. Perhaps where he might have hidden it?"

Papa Joe's face was thoughtful. "I must search my memory. For now, I've given you all that I can."

Frustrated, I toed at the dirt, turning away. "That's not the deal! I solved your riddle. Now it's your turn to give me something—"

I was alone. He'd vanished into the inky darkness.

My mood darkened as a gang of self-defeating thoughts assailed me. *Papa Joe doesn't really want to help me. The journal is probably hidden forever. Hopeless. I'm wasting time.* I recalled when Soc had had me record every passing thought in a small notebook, a form of literary meditation, so that I could become aware of the river of thoughts drifting by. He'd said: "You can't control random thoughts, and you don't need to. Let 'em have their moment, then turn your attention to something worthwhile—like what you're gonna do next."

Okay. So what next? I asked myself.

As I drove back to my motel, an idea came to me. I'd need to pay another visit to Ama at the end of the school day tomorrow.

When I appeared at the door, I found Ama erasing the chalkboard. I smiled, seeing a streak of chalk on her forehead. Abruptly, I asked, "I have something I'd like to try—"

"Dan!" she said, turning to face me.

Her smile invited me to continue. "Would you be open to doing some trance work?"

Brushing back her hair and leaving another white streak on her forehead, she said, "I'm sorry, trance work? You mean hypnosis?"

"It might help you remember more about Socrates."

"I don't think . . ." She took a step back. I realized that I'd been standing very close to her.

"I'm sorry," I said, feeling awkward. "I forget that we've only just met. I wouldn't want a stranger to hypnotize me either."

"It's not that," she said. "It's just that I've never been hypnotized before."

"Some experts," I explained, "think that most people are normally in one or another sort of trance or altered state much of the time—watching a film, reading a book, meditating. Our brain waves change all the time. Mama Chia, a woman I met in Hawaii, worked with *entrancement*, guiding me through visionary experiences to transmit lessons at a deeper level than the intellect. She taught me that the subconscious mind, what she called the *basic self*, takes in more information than the conscious mind can access. If you'll allow me to guide you into a trance state, I'll ask your subconscious mind for impressions, even if they seem unimportant. Whenever you wish to return to your normal state of awareness, you can snap out of it. But it's less abrupt if you let me bring you back."

Ama looked skeptical. Or maybe it was just the sun in her eyes, because she took a seat at one of the children's desks and gestured for me to sit at another.

"Shall we begin?" she said.

"Okay, just get comfortable—that's right, take a nice deep breath. Now let it out. Another. Good. Feel your body grow heavy as you watch my fingertip, up here, just above your eyes."

A few minutes later, in response to my questions, Ama began speaking softly, as if she were talking in her sleep: "I'm sitting next to his bedside. I put a cool cloth on his forehead. His eyes open and he's talking in a kind of reverie, saying: 'I wrote two pages . . . five, ten, twenty . . .'" She crinkled her brow and her speech slowed: "'It came to me . . . felt complete . . . hid it . . . I don't know . . . a safe place.'"

After swaying back and forth in her chair, Ama found a calm space, there in the infirmary of the past. "Now he's sitting up. He looks around the room, then at me. He says something about drinking from the mountain. Or a fountain. I don't know. I offer him water. He sips, then pushes it away. His eyes are open, but he's not awake. He's saying, 'I need to find it.'"

In the voice of a young girl, almost in a whisper, Ama added: "He looks directly at me but doesn't see me. He says, 'It holds a key to eternal life. It shows the way.'"

She sighed, and there was a kind of longing in her voice. "Now he's trying to get out of bed. He seems anxious. He says, 'I might have told others . . . not sure.' Now he's tired, lying back, closing his eyes. Wait, something else . . . about Las Vegas, or nearby. Then he says again the word *mountain* and then *water.* Again I offer him water, which he pushes away and repeats *mountain* and *water*."

Ama sat up so suddenly I thought she'd snapped out of the trance. "A key. I see a key on a table. Then it's gone. . . ."

She went deeper, becoming Socrates, speaking his words, assuming his tone of voice: "'Reminders of higher truth . . . self and no self, death and no death . . . trust in destiny . . . a leap coming . . . have to find it . . . don't know where . . . where am I? Where am I?'"

Silence. A furrowed brow. Then, "'Wait! The sun . . . the sun . . . the sun!'"

I had to presume she was still speaking for Socrates in a sort of empathic connection, dealing with the heat of the desert or the fever. Or both.

It was time to bring her back to everyday awareness. She emerged preoccupied, her eyes wide. "Wait, wait!" she said, sitting absolutely still. Something was pushing at the edge of her memory, about to surface. Then she got it. I could see it in her eyes.

"Dan, about ten years ago, not long before he died, my father's short-term memory began to fail. But his recollection of the distant past astonished me. He had far more to look back on than forward to. So he told me stories when I visited him. Stories about his youth, and sometimes about his patients.

"He recalled not only the feverish man who called himself Socrates, but another man as well—a man who had met my father and then become a sort of patient. . . ."

Again Ama sat and waited, and listened, and searched her own recollection. "I can almost hear my father's voice—how he told me that a few weeks after he had discharged Socrates, another man came to the clinic asking about him, and about some book. My dad couldn't give the man any information, even if he'd known anything, because of patient privacy. So the man left. He seemed disappointed, even distraught.

"That would have been the end of it, but a few months later the man returned, this time pleading with my father for anything he could tell him about the book or its location. To gain my dad's sympathy, and to explain his interest, the man said he was a gardener by trade, had been driving to a job when he chanced upon a man stumbling along the roadway. He couldn't leave anyone out in the midday sun, so he stopped and offered the man a ride.

"He soon realized that the man wasn't drunk but feverish. After accepting a few sips of water, the man muttered in a hoarse voice about a journal he had hidden or lost, and how it revealed a gateway to eternal life. This sounded crazy to the gardener. His impression was confirmed when the deluded man said his name was Socrates. And he claimed to be seventy-six but looked at least twenty or even thirty years younger. The gardener dropped the man off near my father's clinic. That's when Papa Joe must have found him.

"A few weeks later, the gardener was having some odd symptoms and got a medical checkup at a hospital in Albuquerque. He was diagnosed with ALS—Lou Gehrig's disease, a terminal neurological disorder. He was given a prognosis of one to three years. My father said he saw the gardener several times after that. He said he wanted a second opinion, which only confirmed the diagnosis. Then he made appointments just to talk, hoping to learn more about the man Socrates and the journal, clinging to hope. As my dad's role shifted from healer to counselor, he offered what little he remembered hearing from that feverish patient years before. But mostly he just listened.

"The gardener reasoned that if Socrates had stated his age correctly, he might really have found some key to eternal life. By then the gardener had come to believe that he'd been destined to find the feverish man, and that the journal was meant to be his.

"The last time my father saw the gardener, he was frail and had difficulty walking. Now obsessed, he showed my dad notes he'd copied from library books about mystical paths of healing and the search for immortality. About an ancient Persian alchemist who sought to create a catalyst called in Arabic *al iksir* that was said to produce immortality. And Egyptians and Hindus who would ingest certain gems, then sequester themselves in caves or other dark places to wait for a rejuvenation process called *Kaya Kalpa*. The gardener now believed the journal might contain a map to the legendary fountain of youth or to a supernatural mushroom described in some Chinese book or to the philosopher's stone referred to in one of Plato's books, combining earth, air, fire, and water to transform humans into immortals. I recall my dad saying that, delusional or not, the man had done his research."

Ama paused again. "There's something else—oh, yes!—when my father asked the gardener why he was so desperate to live, he said that he needed to survive because of his nine-year-old son. The boy was everything to him. And after his wife had died five years before, he'd raised the boy himself. I think there was an aunt, but . . . that's right—he said the aunt worked nights and slept during the day. . . ." Ama sighed. "I don't think my father ever met the boy, but the son must have witnessed his father losing the ability to make his own food or drive or walk or, at the last, even breathe.

"Six months later, my dad learned that the gardener had died, never having found the man or the journal that he believed might have saved him. But while the gardener could speak, he must have told his son about the man Socrates, and the book that showed the way to eternal life. My dad believed the gardener's son would remember. . . .

"So that's it," Ama said, satisfied, as if she had released a weight from her mind. "The events of this sad story made an impression on my father. I think he told me this story more than once."

In her trance, I thought, *Ama wasn't saying "the sun, the sun!" but rather "the son, the son!"*

Socrates had indeed spoken to a stranger about the journal and what it contained. And the gardener had almost certainly told his son about his quest. *But that was thirty years ago*, I told myself. *The trail has gone cold for decades. The boy has grown up, surely found a life of his own, and he might have moved away and put the past behind him. Probably. Maybe.*

Ama's voice pulled me back to the present. "I thought you should know. It's all I've got. Maybe Papa Joe can add something more. . . . He's unpredictable."

"Yes, I've noticed."

"I think the journal is waiting for the right person—for you, Dan. I hope you find it." We sat in silence for a few minutes more, because there was nothing left to say except good-bye.

As I pulled away from the school, in the rearview mirror I saw two children out in the dusty playground under the oak tree doing cartwheels on the patch of grass. I pulled my eyes away from the mirror and gazed out into the distance, into the unknown.

SEVEN

Sometime later I turned down the dusty gravel path to Papa Joe's shop, intent on asking him about his recent comments and vanishing act. The shop was closed. I waited for nearly an hour before I left, determined to move on. It was unlikely that Papa Joe had anything else to share with me except more riddles. And I was now feeling certain that the journal lay one or two days' travel to the west. Socrates had mentioned both the Mojave Desert and Las Vegas.

After topping off the pickup's oil, I drove west on Route 40 and Route 66, leading toward the badlands of Arizona and eventually the Mojave Desert near the borders of Nevada and California. As I drove, I could picture Socrates dozing in the passenger seat, his feet up on the dashboard. "So, Soc," I said aloud over the rush of hot air through the windshield wing of the dusty pickup, "Am I heading in the right direction? Getting warmer?"—an apt question as the desert oven switched from bake to barbecue. I opened the window and stuck my arm out, but gusts of hot air brought no relief.

The shimmering heat helped me empathize with a feverish Socrates seeking an isolated location to hide the journal well off the beaten path. But the what-if-I-were-a-delirious-Socrates strategy only succeeded in making me thirsty. As the miles rolled by, I passed mesas, cacti, and rolling land. The truck slowly climbed steep grades and then coasted down through a rain-squall in high country before returning to the arid low-lands. As I traveled through the vast spaces of New Mexico and Arizona, I thought of pioneer families making their way through this stretch of inhospitable land in covered wagons.

Meanwhile, I had an eerie feeling that someone was watching me from a distance. I peered ahead through the pockmarked windshield at the long ribbon of road, then glanced into the rearview mirror and out the side windows at the passing scrubland. All I saw were infrequent vehicles and the occasional gas-and-food stop.

Around dusk, I stopped to stretch and relieve myself. Then I drove twenty more miles before catching a few fitful hours of sleep stretched out in the back of the pickup. I rose in the cooling air of the early-morning hours and drove on.

The day dawned hot as I continued west, driving slowly now, scanning the horizon for any promising signs. A mirage on the horizon turned into a real gas station and convenience store. A welcome sight. I pulled in and entered the store.

After loading up on water and a few snacks, I studied a map on the wall, looking for any promising landmarks around Fort Mohave. I noted Las Vegas, about two hours north on Route 95, which passed through the town of Cal-Nev-Ari, named for the three state borders nearby.

I added another quart of oil, and topped off the gas tank and radiator. This old service station, an oasis in the arid expanse, had a special meaning for me, calling forth the many evenings I'd spent with my old mentor back in Berkeley nearly ten years before—like the time Socrates and I had engaged in a heated conversation about the difference between knowledge and wisdom. *Has the world changed,* I wondered, *or have I?* Tapping the dashboard in time to a pop tune on the radio, momentarily lifted by a grander sense of purpose, I eased the pickup back out onto the highway.

Well after dusk, I found a budget motel whose noisy window air conditioner did its best to hold the heat at bay.

Morning was a long time coming. I shook off sleep

with some push-ups and sit-ups until the rising heat made such exertion foolish. I found a pay phone in the hall and called Ama, hoping that she might have recalled some details about the journal's location. When she didn't answer, I called my daughter, listening to the phone ring again and again, reminding myself to send another postcard.

Skipping the motel's continental breakfast—white toast and cornflakes—I continued west.

An hour later, as I checked my map on a long straightaway, a hot breath of wind tore it out of my hands like an angry dog, whipping it out the window and off into the desert. I wasn't about to slam on the brakes and chase it. And what use had it served? Maps were only good for people who knew where they were going.

After a few more miles, I caught sight of a hitchhiker ahead. As I slowed, I saw that he was dressed in a worn suit, even in the desert heat. Pulling over, I rolled down the window. He wasn't as young as I'd first thought, but he wasn't old either—maybe in his midthirties, probably Mexican or mestizo. I sensed a wiry frame underneath his oversize coat. He had a mop of black hair and a deeply tanned face, clean-shaven. "My name is Pájaro," he said with a slight bow.

"And I'm Dan. Would you like a ride?"

He bowed again. "*Gracias*. As long as you are heading in the direction of water."

As the hitchhiker climbed in, I handed him my canteen. He took several modest sips, pouring water into his open mouth without touching his lips to the rim. "You speak English well," I said. "Where did you learn it?"

"Here and there. I made it my business to learn since I'm a businessman."

"What's your business?"

"I buy and sell."

"Anything special?"

"Everything that I sell is special. What I buy—well, that's rather ordinary. As it happens, I'm also a desert guide."

Hmmm, I thought. *A desert guide without any food or water, standing by the highway.* I let the irony settle before asking, "And what do you charge as a desert guide?"

"My fee is nominal and my service exclusive," he explained. "I only take on one client at a time. How about five dollars a day plus food and water?"

"Where do you propose to guide me?"

"Wherever you wish to go. I know every town, every mountain, and every part of the desert," he said without false modesty.

"Every part of the desert?"

"Every one, Señor Dan. I know where the snakes hide, where the dangers lie, and how to find water from the saguaro cactus. . . ."

Why not? I thought. If I was going to play Don Quixote searching for this impossible dream, why not hire a trusted *compañero*? "Okay, Pájaro. It's a deal. For a few days, anyway."

I removed one hand from the wheel, and we shook on it.

"*Pájaro* means bird," he informed me.

We traveled in silence, passing red mesas and foothills as the afternoon pulled the sun toward a distant mountain range.

When the sky to the west turned orange and magenta, I pulled off the dusty road and we made camp. Pájaro suggested a spot that would provide shelter from prevailing winds out of the east or south and offer shade from the rising sun to the east. My spirits rose as sunset brought some relief from the heat. Forewarned about cool nights in the higher elevations, I spread my sleeping sack on a level spot, checking for anthills or other insect activity. Pájaro seemed content to stretch out on his coat.

How different the desert felt when I became a part of it. What looked dead and arid from a distance came alive at night. As a canopy of darkness descended, Pájaro made a small fire. We gazed into the crackling flames. I heard a coyote howl, then two or three more. Pájaro had asked earlier what I was doing in this region; I'd told him only that I was on a personal quest and that I hoped I was heading in the right direction. I gazed up at the star-specked sky. Soon the stars faded into dreams.

The next morning we broke camp early to beat the sun. I figured we'd find somewhere to eat and gas up closer to a populated town. "As it happens, I know a place," Pájaro announced. He directed me to drive due west and, sure enough, after about twenty miles, scattered buildings appeared, then an old gas station adjoining a small café. I knew I needed to find another map despite Pájaro's self-proclaimed mastery of the local geography.

I filled the tank while Pájaro cleaned the windows. I paid him five dollars in advance for the day's services, and extra money to pay for the gas. After he took care of that, he told me he would visit the outdoor restroom, then join me inside the café.

I didn't need a menu: the place smelled of hash browns, coffee, and pancakes. A waitress poured two waters. I drained mine quickly and signaled for a refill.

I looked around at the other diners: A couple. An older woman. A few businessmen on the road. And Papa Joe. Seated at the counter to my left, he dipped a piece of fried bread into a plate of eggs. Shaking my head, I moved over and sat down next to him. He cracked a smile but didn't look up from his food.

"All right, *abuelo*, I have to know. How—"

"Nearly everyone stops here. I can recommend the huevos rancheros."

A few minutes later, I nodded to the waitress as she refilled my glass for the third time, and placed my order. Glancing out the window toward the restroom just outside, wondering what was keeping Pájaro but glad to have some one-on-one time with Papa Joe, I asked, "Can I get you something else to drink? You look as dry as a prune."

"A lemonade will be fine," he said. "And to pass the time as your *huevos* get cooked, I have another—"

I interrupted: "You can only imagine my enthusiasm for yet another riddle paired with almost no useful information."

"I can imagine that and more," he said. "Still, you may learn something useful on the other side of this little mystery: 'I have marble walls as white as milk, lined with skin as soft as silk; no walls are there to this stronghold, yet thieves break in and steal my gold. What am I?'"

"I often wonder about that . . . but let me think: marble walls as white as milk . . ."

"Lined with skin as soft as silk," he repeated.

"Hold on. You said it had marble walls, but later you said that the stronghold had no walls, yet thieves break in to steal its gold. How can there be walls but no walls? And how can thieves break in if there are no walls? It doesn't make any sense!"

"That's why it's a riddle, *burrito*."

The waitress brought the food and I dug in. "It's solvable, though, right?"

"Sure. This is an easy one. The answer is right in front of your nose."

I looked down and took another bite of—of course. "An egg," I answered.

"Thought I might have to cluck and lay one before you got it! But now," he said, finishing off his lemonade with a loud slurp on his straw and setting the glass on the counter with a clunk of authority, "I suppose you expect more information."

"From your vast treasure house."

He leaned conspiratorially toward me and whispered in my ear, "You'll likely find this journal where the hawk soars—in a high place."

"That's it?"

"Well, now you can avoid low places." Glancing left and right as if he could see, as if other ears might be listening, he whispered, "And be selective about where you place your trust."

"Apparently that would include you."

"Of course!" he said with another snaggletoothed smile.

I recalled that Socrates had given me a similar caution years ago, saying that trust had to be earned over time. Meanwhile, Papa Joe gazed through me with his unseeing eyes—an unsettling feeling—and added another caution of his own: "You're in desert country, *nieto*. Pay better attention to what surrounds you than you paid to your meal." With a nod, he slid from his stool and deftly accepted the arm of a passing waitress. I watched as they proceeded outside toward the restroom.

By now it seemed unlikely that Pájaro would be rejoining me. But before he vanished as mysteriously as he'd appeared, he had paid for the gas.

EIGHT

That night I made camp without my desert guide. I took a short night walk by moonlight, hoping the desert might whisper its secrets. Extending my senses into the surroundings, alert to any sign, I glimpsed a rabbit, an owl, and a few lizards. The journal still felt far away.

I got down on hands and knees to watch some fuzzy ants. Just as my face was nearly at ground level, I looked past the ants and saw what they were running from—my first up-close look at a scorpion. Not just any scorpion but, as I later learned from my survival book, a giant desert hairy scorpion, which was ambling in my direction. I jumped up and backed away, my heart pounding as I headed back to camp.

I lay down in my sleeping bag but saw the scorpion again whenever I shut my eyes. That whiplike stinger stirred a memory of the time Socrates referred to my busy mind as a "wild monkey stung by a scorpion." *Maybe it's not the creatures that are frightening me, but my thoughts about them.* Despite the insight, I still jumped up several times, like a wild monkey, to turn my sleeping bag inside out and shake it. Satisfied, I gazed up into the starry firmament, alone in the desert. Just before sleep took me, I heard a coyote and realized: *In the desert, you're never really alone. A thousand creepy-crawlies are out there, waiting.*

In this southern part of the Kaibab National Forest of northern Arizona, a cloudburst could bring out rippling colors: countless arrays of wildflowers splashed with white, yellow, blue, pink, orange, red, and magenta; even the beavertail and prickly pear cacti wore their best. But the heat quickly reasserted itself, increasing my sense of urgency. By the time I crossed paths with an old local at a gas pump, I was feeling so desperate I tried a Hail Mary pass and told him, in faltering Spanish, that I was searching for a *libro particular*, a particular book. He answered, in English, "You can find a nice bookstore back in Flagstaff."

Clearly, I needed to cool off my brain.

The quality of my logic continued to deteriorate as I

cheered myself with such original banalities as: *If you don't care where you are, you're never lost.* Which brought to mind how Socrates would frequently remind me that I was always here, and the time was always now. *And the journal?* I thought. *Always somewhere else.*

Meanwhile, the pickup devoured oil like a drunk on a binge as I chugged past an endless array of cacti and sand drifts, and through a brief downpour that evaporated even before it touched the earth—a local phenomenon called the *virga*, the guidebook said. I reminded myself that sun exposure was the most common cause of death in this area, bringing to mind a visceral memory of my misadventure on a surfboard adrift at sea under a similar blazing sun. *Wherever I turn, death reminds me of Samarra.*

I felt the irrational impulse to pull over, get out my shovel, and start breaking up the soil. I imagined myself as 102-year-old Desert Rat Dan with mummified skin, digging his hundred-thousandth hole. I kept driving.

Alone in the truck, I found my thoughts drifting again and again to the past: a few hundred miles from my current location and seven years past, I was a young college athlete competing in a national championship as if it were the most important thing in the world. I suppose it was at the time, at least to me. Now life had other "importances," as Socrates had once called them—changing values, shifting perspectives.

Other random images and impressions passed through my awareness—Tappan Square Park on the Oberlin campus . . . bodysurfing in the waves at Santa Monica Beach, where I'd come of age—jumbled together with the face of my daughter looking up at me. Then I saw the faces of Ama and then Kimo, a Hawaiian youth who'd shown me the cave beneath the sea where I'd found the little samurai. Which reminded me of Japan, where I'd be right now if I hadn't found that letter from Socrates.

That night I had a crazy dream about my old mentor wearing a string tie, white shirt, and vest—dealing blackjack in a casino! This struck me as so ridiculous that I laughed out loud, waking myself. Still held by the dream, I sat up in my sleeping bag in the cool hours before dawn. I spoke aloud, my throat dry: "No, Soc—you can't be serious!" But according to Ama, Socrates had mentioned that city, or someplace nearby. I couldn't discount any possibility. Vegas rooftops were, after all, high places. Who else but a delirious Socrates would think of concealing a mystic journal atop a hotel casino, hidden in plain sight where no one would look?

Even if the notion was unlikely, I needed a respite

from the dust and heat. So I broke camp, headed north, and checked into a motel a few blocks from the Las Vegas Strip—no luxury resort, but clean, cool, and without an insect in sight.

I dove onto the bed and fell instantly into a deep sleep.

NINE

I awoke the next morning to the maid knocking on my door. "Uh, no need to clean—thanks!" I called out before stepping into a long, steamy shower. Until that moment, I hadn't realized how drained I felt. I shaved and applied a liberal amount of the motel's skin lotion. *When in Vegas*, I thought, *follow the house rules*. (Soc would have approved.)

Outside, I strolled around the swimming pool. *They should put more pools out in the desert,* I thought, making a note to immerse myself soon.

In the motel coffee shop, I drank two glasses of fresh-squeezed orange juice and polished off a fruit salad, an English muffin, and some oatmeal. And a strawberry waffle. Later, I treated the old pickup truck to a wash, watching layers of dirt, grit, and grime slide away. While I waited, I tossed a quarter into one of the omnipresent slot machines in Sin City. The one-armed bandit whirred, the images spun, and when they clicked to a crisp stop, I heard the jingling of quarters—not a lot, but enough to pay for the wash. Maybe my luck was changing.

The Strip was crowded as usual with tourists heading to hotel casinos or wedding chapels promising dreams-come-true. Surrounded on all sides by desert, roasting under a blistering sun, the city if left unattended would soon turn back to dust and sand. While it lasted, it both delivered riches and broke hearts—a place where one could arrive in a $20,000 car and leave on a $100,000 bus.

I decided to take a siesta so I could shift to Vegas time. Like most stylish vampires, the city woke up after dark, making you forget who you were for a little while. But I couldn't afford to forget. Even now, the journal might be nearby, nestled somewhere above my head.

Later, moving through the downtown crowds at 2 a.m., blinking against the lights, I walked through a balmy dreamscape of steel, neon, and deep-pile carpets. Luxurious foliage and fountains conveyed a sense of permanence, but, like much of the town, it was all an illusion.

I drove to the outskirts of the city to view its silhouette, scouting the tallest buildings, where Soc might possibly have hidden the journal. But I couldn't find a single hotel or casino that looked like it would allow rooftop access. So I decided that one or two days of rest and relaxation might refresh my perspective.

I played some blackjack and a little roulette. Twenty dollars ahead, I treated myself to the Mel Brooks film *Blazing Saddles* at an all-night movie theater, forgetting everything else for a few hours of cool air-conditioning and warm popcorn. Back at the motel in the early-morning hours, I stripped down to my underwear (which I figured looked enough like a swimsuit), dove into the lighted pool, and backstroked into the shallows. *What time is it?* I wondered lazily as I bobbed up and down. *Oh right, Soc, I got this one—it's now.*

Late the next morning, fruit juice traveling from a cocktail glass up a straw and into my mouth made me grin—so did floating for an hour on a blow-up raft in the motel pool with the slick feel of sunscreen on my skin. Grinning and giddy. Vegas magic turning one man into an amoeba, undoing epochs of evolution.

Continuing my devolution, that night I found myself at a casino roulette table. I played number eleven—not the smartest move, considering the odds. A modest bet. By midnight and after more losing bets, I still felt a loyalty to good ol' number eleven, so I persisted. It had to come up sometime. Down to my last chips, I heard a whisper: "Put it on sixteen."

I wheeled around—no one nearby but the croupier.

Surely this was a sign. I shifted my remaining stake to number sixteen. The wheel spun and finally stopped—on sixteen! I was about to cash in a sizable pile of chips when the voice spoke again: "Let it ride." So I let it ride. The ball rolled, danced, hovered on the edge of sixteen—then skittered out onto a green zero.

The voice spoke again. And it said, "Damn!"

"Okay, that's it!" I yelled, standing up and glaring at the croupier, whom I held personally responsible for this miscarriage of justice. On the verge of swearing off gambling forever, I gave my last dollar to a slot machine. I had turned to walk away when I heard the clink of enough coins to bankroll a serious duel with the blackjack dealer. I'd caught gambling fever. *Fever!* I thought in a muddled way. *Surely a sign!*

Over the next ten minutes, in a philanthropic mood, I donated nearly two hundred dollars to the casino. This personal largesse and tragedy went unnoticed by the dealer and my fellow players, who were, at the moment, too intent on their own life-or-death dramas to concern themselves with mine.

"I need to remember to bet big when I'm going to win, and bet small when I'm going to lose," I told the dealer.

"Sounds like a good idea," he said.

I doubled down and lost another hand. "You have the eyes of a saint but the hands of an undertaker," I said.

"Amen to that," slurred a man nearby who appeared to be committing financial suicide while his ashen-faced wife watched in horror. I could practically see the coroner's report: death by blackjack.

On the next hand, the dealer had a king showing and a face that revealed nothing else. I had fifteen and, according to the experts, I was supposed to take another card. But I just hate to draw on a fifteen. I tapped the table for another card. Great—an ace. Now I had sixteen. Once again, according to the experts, I was supposed to draw, or odds were I'd lose anyway.

Blackjack, like life, sometimes offers only two choices: bad or worse.

I resigned myself. "Okay, hit me."

The dealer looked at me, puzzled.

"Hit me," I repeated, louder.

He stood there as if he were deaf. "Hit me!" I yelled. So he obliged, throwing a right hook and knocking me right off my stool. I felt my head snap to the side in slow motion as the chair tipped backward, taking me with it.

The instant my head struck the casino floor, I woke up in my motel room.

I squinted at the clock radio on the nightstand: 4:12 a.m. Checking my knapsack pocket, I found my roll of just-in-case travel money still tucked safely away. My gambling-fever dream had a clear message: time to move on.

Before I left, I grabbed an early breakfast, paid my bill, and made a half-hearted attempt to scale the peaks of Las Vegas. In one ascent up my personal Everest, elevator to stairwell to roof, I found a door left ajar, quickly looked around, and found—dare I say it?—*nada*.

Back in the cab of my pickup, I spread out my map.

To the north lay the air force base and gunnery range, which had some high ground. But I wasn't going to dodge artillery shells while peering into small craters.

To the east lay Lake Mead and the Hoover Dam—possible, but not probable (like my life for the past decade).

To the south, Black Mountain and the McCullough Range. That direction looked promising, but just didn't feel right.

To the southwest lay Fort Mohave and Needles, where Route 40 led toward the Nopah and Funeral Mountains, with Death Valley National Monument to the north. What better place to find eternal life than in Death Valley?

I just didn't know. This was a dark night of the soul. Despite my earlier training with Mama Chia, I was starting to doubt my own intuition. What did I have to go on? Even if Soc had pinpointed a single acre, where would I dig? No self-respecting gambler would bet on such a long shot.

I let my hand move across the map. . . .

All at once, two revelations coincided: my hand passed

over a place called Mountain Springs Summit, elevation 5,493 feet, and my neck started tingling. I wasn't sure what that meant, but it meant *something*. It was just an hour outside of Las Vegas.

What did Ama say when she was in that trance? Socrates had repeated something about a mountain and water, but then he'd refused to drink. Maybe he wasn't talking about water but a spring? A mountain spring—or Mountain Springs?

This summit fit Soc's description of a high place. There might be a cave or caves and a view of the desert as a hawk would see it. After meeting young Ama all those years past, he might have made it this far west before his fever overwhelmed him. An image of Socrates hiking up a mountain flashed into my imagination. I could see him sitting on a boulder far from the civilized world, wiping his sweaty brow and writing through his fever with the same penetrating focus and discipline he'd demonstrated so many times back in Berkeley. Then, realizing that he was becoming delirious, Soc could have hidden the journal there, intending to retrieve it later. Another ride or rides might have taken him eastward again, back toward Albuquerque. Perhaps he'd mentioned the last place he remembered. It was a good story. It might have happened that way.

Soc's possible path to Mountain Springs Summit,

then eastward again, made sense only when I considered his confused state of mind. He could have accepted any ride, no matter what the direction. Someone could have dropped him off at the summit. He might then have set out on a path leading upward, away from the road. A quiet place where the hawks could soar. So I would do the same.

TEN

I drove south and then west through this sere land of sagebrush and tumbleweeds. Focused on the road ahead, I dismissed the unlikely notion that someone else might also be seeking the journal. That is until I got a strong sense that I was being watched. *Maybe*, I thought, *it's Soc's gaze I'm feeling.*

Still a jackass, I thought, shaking my head at my own inadequacy as I stumbled around the desert. Maybe a fruitless quest was Soc's way of showing me that I wasn't up to it, that he'd wasted his time with me. He'd shared so much with me, and I, an entitled young college athlete, had assumed I deserved it. How had he put it in his letter? That I believed myself "wiser than my peers." I'd won some competitions, graduated, married, fathered a child, found a coaching job and then the faculty position. What did it add up to now? Who was I but a self-absorbed loner on a fool's mission? If I could find the journal, maybe an answer would lie within its pages.

I reached Mountain Springs Summit in the late afternoon and parked my car off the road. I'd purchased enough food for several days and had filled my canteen, with an extra bottle in reserve. I'd repacked my knapsack, with the small pick sticking out the top. The kachina doll, my little samurai, and my personal journal, with its scattered notes, added bulk. I took them along anyway, not wanting to leave anything important behind.

I gazed up toward a rocky grade a hundred yards away, the only higher elevation Socrates would head for if he was seeking seclusion—if he was ever here at all. I crossed the road and walked to a sort of trailhead. The only path leading upward was bordered on either side by steep walls. This ravine, carved by erosion and time, would be vulnerable to flash flooding and therefore dangerous. But now, under a cloudless sky, it afforded a relatively easy hike up a long stairwell, one small boulder to the next.

As I started up, the sun beat down. It felt like a record temperature until I realized that the heat was internal, like a strange fever. I hoped it wasn't the same kind that had overcome Socrates so long before. Maybe it was my imagination combined with the physical exertion at altitude. I pushed onward and upward.

After a climb of about six hundred feet, the ravine ended in a gentler grade, an expanse of rocky soil. I could see what might be the highest point that would grant me a view of the desert below. A hawk's-eye view. But three paths now lay before me: one on the left, one on the right, and one directly ahead. I had no idea which way to go. Even if Socrates had ascended the same ravine decades ago, which path would he have taken?

A feeling of isolation, even abandonment, washed over me. *Socrates, help me,* I pleaded. *I've never felt so alone.* Meanwhile, my head throbbed.

As the moment of self-pity passed, I took a deep breath and a few swigs of water, splashing some over my hot forehead.

Just then I saw, or thought I saw, a fleeting movement in the distance, along the path to my left. A deer or a mountain goat? I squinted in the sunlight. No, it was a man. I could just make out white hair. Overalls. *In this heat?* I flashed back to a time I had secretly followed Socrates onto the UC Berkeley campus. The figure reminded me of him. Then it disappeared.

I looked toward the path on the right—and saw the figure there. Impossible, but there it was. Then it started to flicker and fade. When I peered up the path directly ahead, I thought I caught a glimpse again. Left, right, straight—each time I looked, the figure was there, and then vanished. My feverish mind strained to figure out what these visions might mean.

I sat down, closed my eyes, and poured more water over my perspiration-matted hair. My teeth chattered with a sudden chill. *How ironic*, I thought. *Here at this high altitude I'm at the lowest point of my life. I don't know what to do, which path to take. . . .* Then I remembered Socrates telling me, "Your analytical skills are useful. So is your intuitive sense of trusting your inner knower. Use both analysis and intuition—but *not at the same time*."

Here and now, analysis would lead me nowhere. This wasn't something I could figure my way out of. I had to trust an inner sense that Mama Chia had helped me refine in the rain forest only a month before. . . . I stood up, closed my eyes, and extended that sense of knowing. . . . I opened my eyes and gazed to the left, to the right, to the path ahead. Three figures of the same man, phantom images of my old mentor. Only this time, two of them flickered and vanished. One remained. The path to the right.

A sage once said, "How do I know what I think until I see what I do?" So I set out, a man on fire, along the path to the right—the right path—acting by faith, not by sight. I could still see the figure in the distance. Sometimes I imagined myself gaining ground. Then he would appear farther ahead. When I reached a level plateau, the figure was gone.

I'd parked the pickup near a roadside sign that read: SUMMIT ELEVATION: 5,493. I'd probably climbed about fifteen hundred feet higher and was now about a mile from the roadway. I heard no sounds here but the wind. Except for the occasional jet streaking across the cerulean sky, I could have been the last person on earth. I stood on a plateau, one of the highest points in miles. Despite the fever and the doubts that possessed me, I sensed that I was getting closer to *something*. If I was wrong, I'd have to go onward, go back, or give up.

Now what? I thought, pacing back and forth across the plateau. That figure—whether real or a daemon Socrates inside my mind—had led me here. But where would I look now? And how could I dig deeper than two inches into this limestone or sandstone surface? *I should have paid better attention in geology class.*

Suddenly tired, my head swimming, I set up camp on the plateau, sweeping away pebbles and laying out my sleeping bag about thirty feet from the cliff's edge. Then I crawled carefully to the precipice, lay on my belly atop a stone outcropping, and peered straight down at a sheer drop of five or six hundred feet. I dropped a stone, which bounced once on a protruding sheet of rock before disappearing into the empty space below. This precarious perch afforded a view of the mountains and desert in the distance.

The sun had nearly set in the west, so I settled in for the night. Huddled in my sleeping bag, alternately sweating and chilled, I asked the universe for another sign. I didn't expect a painted arrow pointing down that said DIG HERE, or a typical omen like the flight of a bird or a gust of wind. I wanted something that would dazzle me.

Funny thing about signs and omens: when you're looking for one, sooner or later it shows up. I didn't have to wait long.

When I awoke in the night, I was lying on my back, facing the starry sky. Then I froze as I saw, in extreme close-up, what had awakened me. My crossed eyes looked past the tip of my nose to see the segmented, armored body of a green scorpion straddling my face. My lips clenched involuntarily, and the tail whipped abruptly into view as the creature stung me right between my brows.

Letting out a shriek, I flailed at my miniature assailant, hitting my own face with such force that I thought I'd broken my nose. My legs tangled with the fabric of my sleeping bag as I tried to climb to my feet, my heart beating so hard I could feel the blood pounding in my head. Watching the scorpion scuttle away, I sat down heavily. It wasn't the sleeping bag that hindered me. I couldn't stand; my legs had turned to liquid, and my forehead started to throb.

My vision blurred, cleared, and then blurred again. I started to shiver, and a wave of nausea passed over me. I alternately sneezed and yawned. My heart felt as if it was skipping beats. I lay back down, fell into a feverish sleep, and tumbled into a place of shadows and shapes undulating in the darkness.

I sat up, or dreamed that I had. The plateau took on a reddish glow. I sprang to my feet, no longer troubled by the scorpion's sting, and wandered around the eerie moonlit landscape. My footsteps made no sound as they fell. A fox appeared out of nowhere, standing not far from the edge of the cliff, and slowly turned its head, its snout pointing toward a lone tree scarred by lightning, before fading into the shadows.

In the next instant, a gust of wind, real or imagined, blew with such intensity that I was knocked off my feet. When I sat up, the lone tree was gone. So was my fever. I walked over to where the fox had stood, less than ten feet from the precipice. To my amazement, the tiny shoot of a plant poked up through the surface of the stone, directly in front of me, and grew rapidly, as if time had sped up. A long, slender, trumpetlike stalk emerged. A thought passed through my mind: *The trumpet announces the coming. . . .*

The top of the stalk opened and blossomed, revealing within its petals an old book—thin, with a reddish leather cover and a metal clasp. Slowly I reached for it. . . .

ELEVEN

I awoke muttering the words, "Thirsty . . . thirsty." Emerging from the dream or vision, I felt my cooler forehead, then reached for my canteen. As I quenched my thirst, the dream monopolized my attention. It had to be here—beneath my feet. But the journal wasn't buried at my feet. It was waiting *in* the mountain, hidden in a cave, like a sacred source of water.

Still feeling shaky from the night's ordeal, I crawled to the cliff edge and peered over once again. Now I knew what to look for. My heart raced as I spied a deep indentation about eight feet below the outcropping—perhaps the entrance to a cave.

Socrates had once said, "In combat and in life, if you start thinking too much, you're dead." The time for action had come. With this resolution, my doubts lifted. I sat for a few moments, breathing slowly and deeply, as Socrates had taught me—not just taking in air but inhaling light, energy, strength. When I felt ready, I shouldered my pack and swung over the cliff edge.

For a few seconds, I dangled precariously on the promontory of rock, the indentation about two feet beneath my boots. I could see clearly from this point that the shadow below was definitely the opening to a cave. Just below the cave entrance was a slight outcropping. If I released my grip, could I land there? My gymnast's instincts said yes.

I started swinging gently back and forth. One more swing, and my fingers released. I arched, and landed on the outcropping. But the weight of the knapsack nearly pulled me backward into space. Throwing my hips forward, I regained my balance, then crawled into the cave, into the mountain.

Exhilarated, I felt my heart pounding like a drum the way it used to in the gym after I'd landed a risky new dismount from the high bar. Scanning my body for any pain or injury, I found none. So I stood up, slightly crouched, and looked around, thinking, *Socrates chose this place, hidden from anyone but birds of prey—where the hawk soars—protected from the weather.*

Dropping to my hands and knees, I crawled forward,

feeling my way deeper into the dimly lit cave. As my eyes slowly adjusted, I saw something resting on a stone shelf. I drew closer. It was the journal. My eyes filled with tears as a mixture of fatigue and elation washed through me, renewing my faith in myself and in the wonder of life. I reached out and clasped the journal with both hands to assure myself it was no illusion. I felt the soul of the ancient woman who'd entrusted it to Socrates so many years before, and something of his soul as well. I hugged it to my chest gently, the way one might hold an infant. I had actually found it.

I allowed myself to savor a few moments of elation, of fulfillment.

I knew that such moments do not last. "Emotions pass like the weather," Soc had once reminded me. That sense of pure joy persisted for about ten seconds.

Now, I thought, *all I have to do is find a way back—*

That's when I realized that I'd been so intent on getting *into* the cave that I hadn't considered how I was going to get *out* of it. It had been relatively easy, if nerve jangling, to drop down; gravity had done most of the work. But now I had to climb out.

Leaving the journal where I'd found it, I crawled back to the cave opening and looked up. Now the outcropping eight or nine feet above, an overhang protruding two feet out from a sheer rock face with no discernible handholds, seemed insurmountable. Maybe impossible.

I wouldn't allow myself to consider that it might be, at least for me, unclimbable. But after pondering it, I had to face the possibility that I could die trapped in the cave, or from a fall while trying to climb out. *A riddle*, I thought. *Okay, what would Papa Joe advise me to do? Or that rascal Socrates, who got me into this fix?*

Postponing a decision, or any impulsive action, I sat at the cave's mouth, my feet dangling over the edge, leaving the journal and knapsack well behind me. I gazed at the panorama before me, watching a hawk soaring in a spiral, riding a thermal updraft in the distance. I reached back and picked up the journal, wondering if it might offer needed inspiration, or the key to getting out—

Where is the key, anyway? I crawled back into the cave and searched the shelf and cave floor, but found nothing.

Thinking the key to my own journal might unlock the old one, I sat down again at the cave's mouth, reached into a side pocket, and retrieved it. My hand trembled with nerves as I tried the clasp. I pushed harder and twisted, which was when my hand slipped. I saw the key fall, bounce once on the stone floor, and sail over the edge. I nearly fell myself, reaching for the key as it disappeared with a sickening finality.

I thought of Papa Joe's words: "You have all the time you need until your time runs out." Had my time run out? *Did I make it this far only to end a few feet short of a future?* I couldn't believe that—I wouldn't! Not with a possible key to eternal life in my hands. (The irony was inescapable—and so, it seemed, was the cave.) In a moment of panic, I began to breathe rapidly.

The next moment I recalled what a navy scuba diver had once told me: In a lapse of good sense, he dove into an underwater cave alone, without affixing a roll of nylon twine outside to use to find his way out again. The dive had looked simple until he found himself in the small cave, having lost sight of the opening through which he could exit. He too began to panic as the cave morphed, in his imagination, into an underwater tomb. His training and a glance at the meter on his air tank calmed him: twenty minutes of air left. He took a slow, deep breath and noticed that his air bubbles were drifting straight down, which meant he was sitting on the ceiling of the cave. He shifted back to the floor, and then slowly swam around the perimeter until the entry/exit hole appeared. He found his way out with ten minutes of air left.

I had plenty of air and abundant time. I only needed a solution. I recalled how a friend once teased me about believing in miracles. "I don't believe in them," I told him. "I rely on them." I needed one now.

So I asked myself a question I had repeated on several occasions over the past decade: *What would Socrates do in this situation?* Then I thought: *Wait a minute—what* did *he do? How could a seventy-six-year-old feverish man have gotten into and out of this place?*

A possible solution appeared, once again, through the agency of a scorpion. I noticed it scuttling along the floor of the cave, marching off into the darkness. I followed, keeping a respectful distance, finding the cave much deeper than I'd first seen. *Socrates couldn't have climbed out! The cave must lead somewhere.*

Of course! The cave had another entrance. And exit. There had to be an easy way out.

Now hopeful, if not giddy, I decided to repack. In the dim light, I carefully removed all of my belongings, and placed Soc's thin journal securely in the pack, followed by assorted clothing, my own journal, the samurai, and the kachina doll. Shouldering the knapsack and holding my flashlight in one hand, I crawled deeper into the interior, moving forward and upward through a narrowing tunnel. Ever on the alert for arachnids.

Cramped spaces were the one thing I enjoyed even less than scorpions and spiders. Now I felt the ceiling descending until the crawl space was so tight that I struggled to remove the knapsack, wrap the straps around my boot, and leave it dragging along behind me for a few yards until the ceiling lifted once more. Relief turned to elation when I saw a distinct pattern of sunlight ahead. Shutting off the flashlight, I scrambled forward.

In one of the great letdowns of my life, I saw that where once a large opening had existed, a pile of boulders now lay. The sunlight I had seen came from a few rays penetrating cracks and crevices, through which I could glimpse an azure sky beyond. The scorpion appeared again, walking slowly past me, exiting through a small opening into the open air. Another opening near chest level allowed me to reach one arm out, but no more. A landslide or cave-in must have occurred in the years since Socrates had hidden the journal.

In a burst of desperate, explosive effort, I tried to dislodge even one boulder, but they were jammed so tight I couldn't begin to move it—even using the pick as leverage. So close and yet so impossibly far! Pounding the boulder, I screamed with frustration.

Then, taking a few slow, deep breaths, I calmed myself, turned around, and returned the way I had come. There was nothing else to do.

Back at the cave opening, I leaned out over the precipice and took another look up the cliff face to see if anything might give me a handhold. I saw nothing.

I still had the pick. I leaned out and swung the pick, but I had little leverage and I could barely see what I was doing. After numerous attempts to chip out a handhold, I looked up and saw that I'd barely even made a mark in the solid stone, about midway to the overhang.

That's when I saw it: what had looked like a shadow about four feet above me in the rock face was an actual indentation that might give me a solid, one-handed grip. If I could pull myself to that point, I might be able to reach up the rest of the way with the pick. I put on the pack and prepared for my final ascent, one way or the other.

Blindly I reached up with the pick again and again until it found the handhold. I pulled. It held. Ever so slowly, I stepped out of the cave and hauled myself upward, hand over hand, climbing the pick's shaft until I was able to squeeze three fingers into the small cavity. Hanging by my left hand, I did a one-arm chin-up. With my right hand holding the very end of the pick handle, I reached up with the pick once again—

The curved steel barely slid over the top of the overhang.

I released my left hand and once again climbed the pick's shaft—slowly, surely, straining every sinew, the weight of the pack pulling me downward. I got one hand over the edge. Now, hanging in space, I released the pick and grabbed the overhang with my right hand as well. I heard the pick clang below, then silence. Drawing on all my remaining strength, I pulled up, got one forearm over, then the other. Fighting for my life, I swung one boot over the edge and scrambled onto the overhang and away from the edge. Panting, I lay facedown on solid rock.

TWELVE

A strange feeling of unreality overcame me. I wasn't sure if I'd ever left the plateau where I now lay on my belly, hugging the ground.

After my breath calmed, I removed the knapsack, clasped it to my chest, and lay on my back, gazing up into the brilliant azure sky. I closed my eyes, savoring another moment, feeling the sun on my face once again.

Then a shadow blocked the sun. A stirring, the trace of a sigh, a nearby presence. With a shock, I opened my eyes and sat up. I turned around and smiled in surprise.

"Pájaro! What in the world are you doing here? How did you—"

"As it happens, I still have the five dollars you paid me, which I'm willing to return in exchange for the journal in your knapsack."

In an instant, it all came into focus: Pájaro was the other man Papa Joe had warned me about. Probably why he'd disappeared when I'd entered that café and found Papa Joe. My instincts weren't wrong. Someone had indeed been watching me. And following me. Pájaro now wore dark, loose cotton pants and a dark, baggy, long-sleeved cotton shirt. And he casually held a pistol pointed in my general direction. The only thought that came to my mind was: *How odd—the Bedouins also wear dark colors, even in the desert.*

Stepping forward, the gun held steady, Pájaro wrenched the bag from me. Without taking his eyes off me, he walked backward about ten feet. "On your stomach!" he said with authority. I lay prone, but kept my head up enough to watch him as he backed up about twenty feet more—to put distance between us, I presumed—before he knelt, turned slightly away from me, and upended my knapsack. I heard, rather than saw, my possessions spill out onto the earth. After looking inside to make sure the knapsack was empty, he tossed it aside. From where I lay I couldn't see exactly what he was doing, but I guessed he was rooting through my clothing, pushing aside the samurai and the kachina doll.

When I started to move, just to shift my weight, he spun back and aimed the pistol directly at me. "Don't," he said.

I didn't.

If he was crazy or desperate enough to kill me, he probably would have already done so. *No need to provoke him,* I told myself, *he can always change his mind.* It dawned on me how vulnerable I was up here atop this lonely mountain, thousands of feet above and miles away from civilization.

My heart sank when Pájaro seemed to find what he was looking for and slipped it into a small pack. He stood, leaving my possessions scattered on the ground. I heard his breathing quicken in excitement.

I would never see that journal again.

He turned back to me. "Where's the key?"

"I don't have it," I said truthfully.

He knelt down again and looked in the side pocket, finding my wallet and a few toiletries. He told me to stand and turn out all my pockets, which I did. Satisfied, he ordered me back to a prone position, then said, "I'm not here to rob you. I'm only taking what's rightfully mine." Then, with the expansive gesture of a victor and a strange air of intimacy, he added, "I'm taking this journal to read at the grave of my father."

The story Ama had told me flashed through my mind. *So it's true,* I thought. *He's the gardener's son!* In a moment of compassion, I pleaded with him, for my sake and for his: "Don't do this, Pájaro! It's a mista—"

As I started to lift up my head, I glimpsed a flash of motion. Then the world exploded into darkness.

I awoke with a throbbing head and felt a large lump. Now alone, I crawled over to the spilled knapsack, hardly believing that he'd left it all—clothing, canteen, my wallet, even the five dollars he owed me. All but the journal.

I still couldn't quite bring myself to look. Not knowing, I still had hope. But I couldn't delay any longer. I reached deep into the empty sack and gasped as I felt Soc's thin journal through the tear in the lining. For safekeeping, I'd secured it behind the lining when repacking. I'd done so by instinct rather than forethought.

When Pájaro turned the pack upside down, it had only lodged more securely behind the lining. He had expected, and seen, a heavier journal, locked with a clasp. The thin volume would have felt like little more than a cardboard reinforcement at the back of the pack.

My hand emerged, holding the book in the desert, passed on to Socrates by Nada so many years before, now safe in my keeping.

But not for long if I lingered there.

Pájaro had taken my personal journal containing nothing but a few scattered notes of my travels. How long would it take him to reach his father's gravesite? It might even be somewhere nearby. Or he might have pulled over, consumed by curiosity, and cut the strap.

I had to move quickly. How would he react when he discovered that I had somehow deceived him?

Still shaken, I shoved my belongings back into the pack, then managed to stand and then walk, breaking into a stumbling run down the mountain.

On the chance that I might recover quickly and follow him, Pájaro had slashed two of the pickup's tires. Abandoning the truck, I hiked down a thousand-foot grade to another road and waited for the longest thirty minutes of my life until a trucker heading west picked me up. Relieved, I told him that dinner was on me at the next truck stop, then slid down in the seat as if taking a nap. I was exhausted and my head still ached, but I was far too nervous to sleep. I stayed out of sight of any passing cars and focused on the road ahead.

It was time to leave the country.

THIRTEEN

At the next truck stop, I gave the driver money for his meal and a quick handshake, then excused myself. At a pay phone outside, I placed a call to the rental company, reporting the vandalism and the location of the pickup, and said I'd found other transportation. Then I called the airline and arranged to leave LAX for Japan the next day. I thought of calling my daughter, and then Ama, but decided that would have to wait. Right now I needed to catch a ride.

I asked several people on their way to their cars if they were headed toward Los Angeles. After several head shakes, a hefty bearded guy opened the door of a late-model Chevy Camaro and nodded. I sighed with relief as we pulled out, but every time we passed a car, I slid a little lower in my seat, which seemed to amuse my driver. "Sticking it to the man?" he asked.

"Something like that."

Like the Camaro, my mind went into overdrive as we sped out of desert country and approached Los Angeles County. I had to assume that Pájaro—the gardener's son—would be seeking me by now, or soon.

When my ride dropped me off a few miles from LAX the next morning, I walked to a nearby hotel entrance to catch a taxi. I found momentary satisfaction in paying the driver with the five-dollar bill Pájaro had left on the ground next to me after knocking me unconscious.

After checking in and getting my boarding pass, I bought another folding knife, a new notebook, two pens, a baseball cap, a T-shirt, a small towel, and a few other small items. I put my wallet, my passport, Soc's letter, and about $180 in remaining cash in a smaller pocket of the knapsack. I checked to make sure the journal was still safely tucked under the lining.

In a nearby restroom I removed my sweat-soaked shirt and stuffed it into the trash. I pulled on a new pair of socks and washed the dirt from my hiking boots. After cleaning my face, chest, and underarms, I slipped into the tourist T-shirt, strung the sunglasses around my neck, and donned the baseball cap.

Now less recognizable and with all my belongings repacked, I heard the boarding announcement for my flight. I rushed to the gate, abandoning plans to call my daughter or Ama for now. Vigilant, if not slightly paranoid, I kept looking over my shoulder and scanning the concourse and the crowd of other travelers at the gate.

I boarded the flight, which would connect through Hong Kong and then continue, finally, to Japan. Finding my seat, I forced myself to stay awake until the airplane door closed and we started to taxi. Then with a sigh and a comforting thought—*If I don't know my next address, he can't either*—I fell down the rabbit hole of sleep.

I awoke in darkness with a start. It took me a few moments to recall where I was. From the window seat, I glanced at the two passengers on my right. Both were asleep. I pulled my knapsack from under the seat. Carefully removing the journal, I stared at the metal clasp. It had a slot for an old-fashioned key. Socrates must have had the key. Why hadn't he left it with the journal? I tried picking the clasp with my knife without success. I could cut the short strap, but something stopped me. It wasn't like breaking into a pharaoh's tomb, but it didn't feel right. I pulled again at the clasp. It held fast.

I slipped the journal back into my knapsack and was about to drift off again, trusting my subconscious to come up with a solution. Almost as soon as I closed my eyes, the kachina doll appeared in mind, along with Papa Joe's words: "I've given you all that I can." Then I thought, *It's a gift for my daughter, nothing more.* Still, I reopened the knapsack and reached past shirts and underwear to retrieve the doll. I felt the round base of the doll and found a soft spot. I turned it over and pushed. The paper tore in a semicircle. I shook the doll, and an old key, wrapped in a strip of paper, fell into my hand. On the scrap of paper I could just make out one word, in a shaky script: *¡Exactamente!* I retrieved the journal and fit the key into the lock. The clasp opened.

Socrates must have given the key to Papa Joe for reasons of his own. Or Papa Joe had taken it. Either way, he had chosen to give the key to me. I felt a warm glow toward the old man. And toward Ama too. I'd call her soon and tell her what had happened.

As the aircraft soared over the Arctic Circle, I opened the first page of the journal to see the text that Socrates had already shared in his letter. I read the story again, written in Nada's hand, about the flight to Samarra. I wondered, *Is Samarra a place or a reminder to us all?*

I turned the page, flipped through the slim book, and saw that Socrates had indeed written on about twenty pages, leaving nearly as many blank. But the fever had taken its toll: instead of the lucid text Soc's letter had led me to hope for, I found broken phrases, insights, and notes. If a coherent thread had unspooled from his subconscious, it wasn't yet visible to me. What I found was more outline than polished thesis. It was almost as if Socrates had laid the groundwork for someone else to build upon. Someone like me.

I felt a wave of adrenaline followed by a sinking feeling (or maybe it was the other way around), perhaps not unlike the feeling Soc had described having when he read Nada's note encouraging him to fill in the blank pages.

The torch had now been passed to me. A strange thrill snaked up my spine—a sense of déjà vu—as I realized that the ancient Greek Socrates was an oral teacher. It was his own student and colleague, Plato, who committed his teacher's ideas to the written word. *But I'm no Plato!* I thought.

I would need to study what Soc had written. I'd have to read it many times, memorize all of it, and then let it settle into me and shape itself. And then, just maybe—drawing on all my training with him—I could apply my own discernment to expand on his insights, filling in where necessary, interpreting, and finally writing something worthy of his wisdom. Now I knew the kind of responsibility that Socrates must have experienced in facing those empty pages. Then I fell into a deep sleep and didn't wake again until the wheels touched down in Hong Kong.

During our long taxi to the terminal, the captain announced, "Due to a maintenance issue, we'll have a delay of around four hours. Feel free to deplane, but stay close to the boarding area." That's when it occurred to me: *What if*

I don't reboard? What if I stay here and explore the city? An unscheduled stop wouldn't hurt. Besides, Hong Kong was well-known for practitioners of t'ai chi and other internal arts from China. I could visit some local teachers, inquire about schools off the beaten path. Another long shot, but I seemed to be depending on those lately. I might even drop the name Socrates, here and there. I notified the airline, cleared customs, and walked out of the airport.

PART TWO

The Master of Taishan Forest

All human beings should try to learn, before they die,
what they are running from, and to, and why.

JAMES THURBER

To be blessed in death, one must learn to live.
To be blessed in life, one must learn to die.

MEDIEVAL PROVERB

FOURTEEN

Unable to sleep due to a mix of excitement and jet lag, I walked through the thick air of darkening streets, now empty except for a few vendors hosing or sweeping the sidewalks, by clothing-shop windows featuring SALE signs in English and Chinese characters, and past jewelers, banks, and a movie house whose marquee featured a new Shaw Brothers film, *The Spiritual Boxer*. This time of night the city felt like a large jewel box slowly shutting.

Near dawn I found myself on a wharf overlooking Victoria Harbor and saw the ferry pushing through black water, distorting the reflected lights of the modern city beyond. I stood there waiting for a sign. *Something small,* I thought, *so I'll know I made the right decision.*

A paper cup floated by, then a cigarette butt. Not much by way of omens.

As the sun rose, I returned to my tiny room, intent on studying Soc's journal notes, but I fell asleep with my hand on the cover and slept through most of the day.

When I awoke in the early afternoon, I bought and mailed another postcard for my daughter at a tourist kiosk. I would have made the expensive phone call to her, but I wasn't sure whether she and her mom were still in Texas or on their way back to Ohio. So postcards would have to do for now. I still wanted to call Ama; it seemed I owed her that for her help. But the time difference made it more difficult.

I found a few random Chinese martial arts schools advertising Shaolin Temple Boxing, Top Kung Fu, T'ai Chi Chuan, and Qigong for Health. I sensed little of the "mysterious East" except that the few students I saw were all Chinese. I was able to speak with one instructor during a smoking break to ask (feeling like an idiot) about any "hidden school" he might have heard of; in reply, he told me some myth about an ancient school in his tradition.

None of the other schools I found held more than passing interest. I wrote some notes about the martial arts I'd observed for my report to the grant committee, in between walking down side streets and alleyways, inhaling the exotic aromas of unfamiliar foods. I would turn right or left on instinct or impulse.

During these token searches, without much hope of finding anything out of the ordinary, I remained preoccupied with the task that had fallen to me. *When will I begin writing?* Meanwhile, Socrates had directed me to find a hidden school in Asia. Which I believed might be in Japan. *So what am I doing here?* Different voices in my head, none of which felt quite like my own.

Eventually I circled around to Kowloon Bay, which geographically separated Hong Kong from the People's Republic of China—Mao's China. I had no wish to visit a place where I'd be viewed as "an imperialist running dog," barking and wagging my tail much like the Disney dog Pluto, which reminded me of Plato, which reminded me of the journal awaiting my attention.

I spent another day crisscrossing the downtown and the city outskirts, passing places I'd been before. I'd clung to a hope that this search might bear fruit as had another search in Hawaii four weeks earlier. But those tropical isles seemed far away and long ago, and Japan remained a hope, an idea, a point on the map. My only reality was here and now, and I had to face that it wasn't so promising.

That night I spied a cockroach ambling across the wrinkled bedsheet. I flicked it off the bed; it landed, righted itself, and continued on unperturbed. *Will it outlive me?* I wondered. I'd already met a variety of marching insects and their cousins, all of which demonstrated a better sense of where they were going than I had. *If only I were an imperial running dog*, I mused. *I might be able to sniff out some possibilities*.

I stared up at the cracks in the ceiling. A window fan went *ticka-ticka-ticka* as it blew thick, warm, malodorous air down at me—the window looked out on garbage piled in the alley. The city of Hong Kong, like most, changed faces for different visitors. Mine was the Hong Kong of a budget traveler, a professor-vagabond who'd lucked into a great job in a small college town far, far away as the *ticka-ticka-ticka* fan of my life spun crookedly onward.

The next day just before dawn, I decided to take one last walk through a local park before heading to the airport. In the distance, I saw a handful of people practicing the slow-motion movements of t'ai chi. The thought occurred: *What if the hidden school is really outside?* I didn't give it much credence, but there was no harm in getting a closer look. I chose a good vantage point, squatted down, and observed.

It wasn't unusual to see early-morning practitioners of t'ai chi in a public park. I would soon have moved on, but one woman caught my eye. She moved with a grace and precision unusual for a woman in her middle years. Or for anyone. She had a catlike quality that reminded me of Socrates. Could she be a master hiding in plain sight?

Briefly our eyes met as she continued the effortless-looking movements I recognized as the traditional Yang form. But she amplified and refined it. I'd practiced sufficient t'ai chi to grasp the basic form, and to discern expertise when I saw it.

As the last star melted away with the sunrise, she began the form again, this time on the opposite side—a mirror reflection that I could follow. So, on impulse, I approached and began to mimic her movements. Soon I was immersed in the relaxed yin-yang flow, shifting weight from one leg to the other, turning from the core, releasing tension as it arose. For the moment, past and future receded. . . .

I was completing an element called Single Whip when I felt the lightest touch between my shoulder blades. The next thing I knew I was hurtling forward and rolling on the sparse grass. I leapt up and spun around. My eyes turned first to my knapsack, still secure, then darted around in search of the assailant who had sent me flying. Picking up my pack, I moved through the group, asking anyone nearby, "Who pushed me?" Most of them, immersed in their moving meditation, ignored me. Then I heard a giggle.

When I turned, I saw the woman I'd been watching. A head shorter than I, with short, dark hair streaked with white, she mimicked the stance of an American teenager, one hand on the cocked hip of her tracksuit pants. "Why, *I* pushed you, of course," she said in British-accented English. "What're you going to do about it?"

"What—? How—? You pushed me? Uh, why?"

"You sound like a journalist," she quipped, both hands now on her hips, "but you've left out *where* and *when*. As to *why*? To provide a basis for conversation."

"How do you know I want to have a conversation with you?"

"Don't you?"

"Well, maybe," I said. *Of course I do!* I thought. "So how did you send me flying? I barely felt a tap."

"Isn't there an American joke . . . ?" she said. "A young musician visiting Manhattan asks a local how to get to Carnegie Hall—"

"Practice, practice, practice," I said.

"Ah, you've heard it," she said, a little disappointed. "Then you know the answer to your own question. I've practiced sincerely for many years, just as you've practiced acrobatics."

"How do you know that?"

"A trained eye. Anyway, it's pretty obvious, don't you think? You roll better than you stand. And you seem more connected to the clouds than rooted to the earth."

"Fair enough. Let's start over." I introduced myself and told her my official purpose for being here.

She shrugged, unimpressed. "I'm called Hua Chi. And

since you're here to observe"—she pointed to a young woman who also showed superb skill—"why don't you take a closer look at my student Chiang Wei's movement?"

"Your student?"

"Yes. As your American pundit Yogi Berra once said, 'You can observe a lot just by watching.'"

I squatted down again next to my knapsack and watched Chiang Wei demonstrate paradox in motion: soft yet powerful, rooted yet weightless, as she leapt and spun with circular blocks and kicks. I listened for the sounds of her feet touching the earth but heard none.

When she and her companions finished the form, they bowed toward Hua Chi in the traditional manner, covering a fist with the palm of the other hand, and hurried off. I had the impulse to follow Chiang Wei and her friends, but instead I went to stand by Hua Chi—at a respectful distance.

"Please join me at my home," she said. "We'll have tea and conversation. I want to know what Americans are watching on television these days." An unexpected comment. *She's full of surprises,* I thought. I had no idea how true that was.

Just like that, I had somewhere to go, someplace to be. A contact. I could always catch an afternoon flight.

The swarms of people walking and bicycling in every direction reminded me of a movie set—I half-expected a director to shout "Cut!" at any moment as I did my best to follow Hua Chi's tiny figure through the crowds. In a variation on t'ai chi practice, we navigated our way through the crowds, sidestepping garbage here, passing a noodle stand there, and sliding through a flood of people entering and exiting a government office.

Farther from the city park on a smaller street, several workers were building a wall with hard-packed loess, a common kind of yellow sediment, which covered the workers' hair and turned to grime on their bare backs. I barely managed to stay a few steps behind Hua Chi as nearby shops opened with a clatter of locks. The city's jewel-box lid opened once again.

Finally catching up, I asked: "Excuse me, Hua Chi, but isn't it unusual to invite a foreigner over for tea?"

"I suppose. But you're the first foreigner I've seen practicing t'ai chi in the park so early in the morning."

We rounded a corner, then stopped. "Home," she said, pointing to a green thicket across the narrow street. An array of white and purple flowers lined a leafy wall. Only when we had crossed and stood directly in front of it did the entrance appear: an angled archway set so low I had to stoop to follow her. I duckwalked down a tunnel fragrant with bright red chrysanthemums. The perfumed archway twisted and turned like a maze until we stood in front of a small three-room house.

Removing my shoes as Hua Chi did, I entered and sat on the floor in front of a low table while she set a teapot on a small stove. I waited in silence, marveling at her decorative scheme of organized chaos: everywhere I looked I saw international artifacts—newspapers in multiple languages; colorful tchotchkes, including a miniature plastic Yogi Berra; cassette tapes; rolled-up movie posters; and piles of T-shirts with bizarre slogans in English and French. I heard the water boil. Soon after, she poured the steaming water over green herbs taken from a small disco ball, the two halves of which squeaked as she screwed them back together.

"I work in the travel industry," she said, following my gaze. "I collect this and that."

After we'd taken a few sips of aromatic tea, Hua Chi spoke again. "Tell me about your favorite television shows."

"Really? Well, I . . . don't really watch much TV at home. But there's one show I never miss. It's called *Kung Fu*—"

Her eyes lit up with the enthusiasm of a three-year-old. "Really? It's also my favorite! In fact, I have something of a crush on Kwai Chang Caine."

"But he's not even Chinese!" I said. "You know, Bruce Lee wanted to play that role—"

"Lee was a talented martial artist. I greatly admired

him and I mourn his death," she said. She was silent for a moment, then added, "David Carradine is *the man*, don't you think?"

"Yes, a peaceful warrior—when he's not kicking ass," I noted, before blurting my thoughts aloud. "I can't believe I'm sharing a fan moment with a t'ai chi master in Hong Kong!"

Hua Chi shifted gears so abruptly she seemed an entirely different person, now calm and serious. "On rare occasions, I meet someone who may be ready to learn, and who may also have experience to share."

"You mean me? Why would you think I have something to share?"

"Something in your eyes and your posture," she said, "an uprightness. I'd say you've studied with a master teacher."

"I did—I do—have a mentor. But I've trained in gymnastics more than in the martial arts."

"So I've noticed," she said, unable to suppress a smile. "Your path, your tao, is that of the acrobat. As it should be. After all, does the flame aspire to become fallen snow? Does the rose grimace like a raccoon?" She raised a hand, her finger pointing to the heavens, and said, "The wise master their own path in their own way."

"Is that from Confucius?"

She smiled. "Nope. Master Po—*Kung Fu*." Hua Chi rose and, pushing aside various paraphernalia, she seized one of the poster tubes, which she unrolled to show David Carradine's face in extreme close-up. She stroked the actor's cheek.

I thought back to Papa Joe's similar reference only a few weeks before. Hua Chi tossed the poster aside and a moment later sat opposite me again, looking serious once more.

"My mentor, whom I call Socrates after the Greek sage, once told me that while I practice gymnastics, he practices everything."

Hua Chi nodded approvingly. "Indeed! Each path can become a way of life. The small tao merges with the Great Tao as many streams merge with a great river."

"*Kung Fu* again?"

"No, that's a Hua Chi original."

"There's something else," I said. "I'm here on a personal quest. Socrates sent me to find a journal containing his insights. I've found it. I have it with me."

Seemingly ignoring my comments, Hua Chi shifted toward the existential: "Isn't it intriguing that when we rose this morning, neither you nor I had any knowledge of our meeting? Yet here we are. Who knows why you came to Hong Kong Park on this particular morning at that particular time? Who knows why I was moved to give you a push . . . in the right direction?"

My memory leapt to the odd circumstances surrounding my first meeting with Socrates, late one night in that old service station. Following my impulse to enter his office had not only changed the course of my life, but also made me a lifelong believer in trusting my "inner knower"—even if intuitive impulses sometimes led me on a winding path. Might my meeting with Hua Chi be another such moment? I almost missed what she said next: ". . . willing to apply yourself, I may be able to arrange some training in line with your interests."

Considering her offer, I thought: *A few weeks of training with Hua Chi before catching my next flight. Why not?*

"That's very generous," I said. "Would we train here or in the park?"

She laughed. "No, Dan. Not here, and not with me. There's another master who can better serve your needs. You'll need to make a journey to my brother Ch'an's farm. The young farmworkers there—nearly all are orphans—also practice t'ai chi under the watchful eye of— Well, you'll learn that soon enough. I can't speak for the master, but if you're willing to work the land with the other students, the master may be willing to instruct you as well. For reasons of peace and politics, it's hidden deep in a forest."

A hidden school? I thought, not certain I'd heard correctly. "My mentor encouraged me to find such a school. . . ."

Hua Chi refilled my cup, "So you were looking for *a* school, and now you've met me. What an interesting coincidence," she said. "If you believe in such things."

"Coincidence or not," I said, cradling my cup carefully, "I'm ready to visit this Master Ch'an anytime you are."

Hua Chi rose to her feet—or rather, floated upward—and moved across the room to another low table, where she pushed aside a pair of bell-bottom jeans and opened a drawer. "One doesn't just drop in at this particular place. It's a long journey to the Taishan Forest. It's located in northeast China—"

"China?" I thought I must have misunderstood. "Mao's China? But I couldn't . . . I don't have—"

"I'll need to write letters of introduction and arrange for your passage." She reached into the drawer and brandished a small pot of ink, a calligraphy brush, and some rice paper.

"How will I clear border security?"

"There will be no security where you're going. Come back in two days, right after dawn. I'll have made the necessary preparations. You'll need to travel light—"

I pointed to my knapsack.

"Good," she said, sitting down to write. The Chinese

characters flowed from her brush as if her hand were ice-skating on the parchment.

"I really appreciate—"

"You'll earn your keep," she murmured. Without looking up, she batted away a Mickey Mouse balloon as it floated near her head. "Meet me back here in two days. Same time."

FIFTEEN

As I bowed in farewell, Hua Chi was so focused on writing that she barely acknowledged me. But before I left, I said, "The journal I mentioned. There might be another man seeking it, for reasons of his own. He could be dangerous. It's highly unlikely he'll follow me or find me here. But just to be safe, I thought I'd mention it."

Hua Chi barely seemed to be listening but said absentmindedly as she wrote, "How dramatic. I wonder what Kwai Chang Caine would do?"

With another bow, I took my leave through the low trellis of flowers, a tunnel between worlds. I liked Hua Chi for her skill and charming eccentricities. But could I trust her? As I found my way back the way we'd come, I wondered what I was getting myself into. Was I prepared to let her arrange my transit into the People's Republic of China, where zealous cadres of the People's Liberation Army might question any foreign traveler?

The answer was yes. A door had opened. I would walk through it, into another world, and see what would unfold. In the meantime, I tried calling my little girl one last time, both at the number she had given me in Texas and back home in Ohio. No luck reaching her. Or Ama.

I spent the next two days in my room or at a local park, studying Soc's notes, letting his words penetrate me—until finally I sat again at Hua Chi's low wooden table, sipping tea. She handed me some papers. "Keep them safe," she said. "It can be difficult sparring with bureaucrats, but a few friends and relatives in positions of authority can move mountains."

"Why do I need a letter when you'll be—?"

"I have obligations here. I'll join you later this month or the next. As soon as I can."

"But I assumed—"

"Assume nothing," she said, "especially in China, given the current political climate." To her, I supposed, politics were temporary, but pop culture lived forever.

I unfolded the rice paper and saw a letter in Chinese calligraphy, with brief instructions for me in English, which she proceeded to repeat aloud: "Show these to the boat captains. *Show* the letters, but keep them in your possession." To emphasize her instruction, she slapped the papers out of my hand and pushed them against my chest.

Everything happened quickly after that. On our way to the dock, as I hurried after Hua Chi through the crowded streets, she gave her final reminders: "Even after your President Nixon's visit," she cautioned me, "a foreigner is viewed with suspicion and could even be arrested as a spy. Don't draw attention to yourself! Remain quiet and friendly. Make no disturbance. Keep to yourself whenever possible. You're young and strong, but fate is a jester."

"What will I say to Master Ch'an when I meet him?" I asked, striding rapidly to keep up with her as we neared the docks. "How do I know he'll even accept me as a student?"

"He speaks only Mandarin, so you won't speak directly to him. Someone will translate—a woman. But if you reach the school, you'll be welcome."

If I reach the school? Had I heard her correctly? There was no time for pondering or reassurance; the captain of the fishing trawler nodded curtly to Hua Chi and motioned me aboard. I felt the engine's vibration.

Then I suddenly remembered—I'd intended to call Ama one last time before I left, but in the sudden rush I'd forgotten to do so. I quickly grabbed a pen and wrote Ama's name and number on a piece of paper. Stretching out from the boat, I handed it to Hua Chi.

As the boat began to pull away, I shouted over the thrumming engine. "Please, call this woman! She needs to know I found the journal!"

Hua Chi smiled and waved as if I were only saying good-bye. I heard her say, "Good journey, Dan. And don't forget—"

Her voice was lost as the engines turned to full power. I yelled out, "Don't forget what?" But my words fell into the sea.

It wasn't until later that I realized we'd never discussed how I would arrange my return trip. Only that she'd join me when she could.

Seized by a mixture of anticipation and dread, I stood on deck and watched the shoreline disappear into the haze. *What have I done?* I wondered, gazing at the map she had drawn. I'd embarked on a one-way journey by sea, then river, followed by a trek through Russian territory into China to find Mount Tai and the Taishan Forest in its foot-hills, where I might or might not find a school.

I felt a tap on my shoulder. The captain held out his hand. I thought he was gesturing for money, then realized that he wanted to see the letter. He grabbed it from my hands, read it, and gave a tight-lipped smile, bobbing his head. Still holding the letter, he said something and ges-tured for me to follow him to a small room, the size of a closet. I saw a bunk and a small washbasin. My sleeping quarters. He pointed to another room near a cooking stove, presumably where I'd eat with the crew. Last, he led me down the gangway to another door, where the odor told me the purpose. Then he waved me away, and walked off with the letter!

When I caught up to him on deck, he'd already put it away. I spoke and gestured, trying to make him understand that I wanted the letter back. As he called out to the crew, his attention elsewhere, he reached into his jacket and returned the now-wrinkled sheet of rice paper that I'd need to show to the next captain.

According to Hua Chi, my eventual destination was the Taishan Forest in the Aihui District of the Heihe region—a supposedly isolated woods in an otherwise populated area. When I showed the map to one of the sailors, he traced our route northward through the East China Sea, passing between mainland China and Taiwan to the east.

Over the next few days, we motored past South Korea and up into the Sea of Japan, moving due north from there. During our voyage, the ship anchored several times to fish, dropping the catch into an ice-filled hold. When we docked at each of several ports, I retreated to my cabin, awaiting a signal from the crew (when they remembered to give it), after which I was again free to wander the decks.

Somewhere on an isolated inlet of South Korea, I disembarked without ceremony. About ten minutes later, I was met by a gray-haired man who took me to the next captain Hua Chi had mentioned, a man named Kim Yun. I handed him the letter. He glanced at it, frowned at me, tore it up, and walked away, boarding his ship. Dropping to my knees, I gathered the shredded letter and followed him up onto the boat, babbling. "Why? What's wrong? Hua Chi—"

At the sound of her name, the captain turned again. He clearly didn't understand anything else of what I was saying. The gray-haired man appeared at my side. In broken English, he said, "Show me," gesturing to the fragments of the letter. Reading what he could, he said, "Not letter." He spoke sharply to Kim Yun, who said little in return, but apparently they came to an agreement.

The gray-haired man turned back to me. "You work, he take you," he said, miming what looked like mopping the decks.

About to protest, I shut up, thinking, *Why not?* I'd done practically nothing resembling simple labor since I'd left Oberlin months before. Something about the idea energized me. I quickly nodded. Moments later, my gray-haired Good Samaritan was gone, and I was pulling away from the shore once again.

Either my initial mopping was clumsy, or the captain

changed his mind; during the three days I spent on the second boat, no one asked me to do any work beyond that first round, much less swabbing the decks, though I bunked with the crew this time. For the most part, they ignored me as if I were a ghost.

Only one good thing came out of the experience: alone in the crew quarters, once again drifting through time and the sea, I had time to take out Soc's journal and study his fragmented thoughts and commentary. Despite the occasional full sentence or even paragraph, he'd mainly scrawled phrases in an outline of insights I'd have to make sense of before I could expand upon them. A larger theme gradually began to take shape in the pages of my mind. It was something that had begun when I'd first met Socrates. Back when I was a college athlete who would rather attempt dangerous new moves than write an essay.

I couldn't do any real writing now; the seas were too rough, and wielding a pen made me seasick. But the time would come after I reached the school. This period at sea forced me to contemplate before I began writing. So as I lay curled on my bunk, feeling the swell of each wave, I watched thoughts and ideas congeal like planets formed from stardust. And I began to see . . . Soc had indeed found a way to "attain eternal life." Not in the sense that many might imagine or hope for, but in a way nonetheless.

The sound of footsteps woke me. My hand found the journal before I opened my eyes. A nod from a crew member told me it would soon be time to disembark. I organized my knapsack and hurried up on deck just in time to see us motor past the port of Vladivostok, Russia.

I couldn't disembark at the port, which would have required a visa. But forty-five minutes due north, at an isolated coastal inlet, I left the boat at a small Russian outpost, little more than a hut selling basic supplies. I traded a few American dollars for enough Russian rubles to purchase food, a compass, another canteen, and a cap with a red star. In the interest of traveling light, I'd abandoned my desert sleeping sack for a tarp I could pull over me if needed. I also managed to acquire some Chinese currency even though Hua Chi had told me I wouldn't need money during my journey or at the school.

She'd advised me to avoid populated areas—"Tighten your belt and push on!"—which I intended to do. There would be food enough, and rest, when I reached the farm or school or whatever it was. *If* I reached it. *Am I crazy to trust her?* Socrates had once advised me, "Trust should not be given quickly—it has to be earned over time." I knew next to nothing about Hua Chi except that we shared a fondness for a television show and for t'ai chi. *She could be sending me to some prison cult,* I thought, *a Chinese* Heart of Darkness *or a scenario straight out of George Orwell's* Animal Farm.

In the brief time we'd spent together, however, Hua Chi had impressed me as sincere. I couldn't fathom why she showed such interest in helping a visiting professor, but could anyone ever be certain about another's motives?

SIXTEEN

With a map, a compass, and Hua Chi's directions to guide me, I hiked into a Russian woodland, heading toward the eastern shore of Lake Khanka. Crossing rough, thickly forested terrain, taking shelter during the occasional rainsquall, I traveled two days to reach the lakeshore. I skirted populated areas but caught glimpses, in more rural terrain, of peasants knee-deep in rice paddies—men and women working side by side, plowing with oxen under sapphire skies tinted with layers of yellow dust. A few sheep grazed on small patches of arid land.

Thankfully, I saw no military or police officials. I continued north until I found the mouth of the Ussuri River, marking the border between China and Russia. That's where the river-going flatboat and her captain found me pacing when they showed up three hours after our appointed time.

Fortunately, this captain didn't care that I had no letter—only that I held out the right denomination of Chinese currency. He took me upriver for a day to where the Ussuri met the broad river called Amur by the Russians and Black Dragon by the Chinese, as Hua Chi had told me. We made our way north until I disembarked abruptly when the captain nearly pushed me and my knapsack out of the boat, then pulled away.

Now I was truly in the middle of nowhere. The boat disappeared, taking with it the comforting *chupa-chupa* of the engine. If I were injured or incapacitated, I could die here. And if I died, my young daughter would never know what had happened to me. Socrates would never learn I'd found the journal. *So you'd better not die!* I told myself.

On the brighter side, Pájaro could never, ever track me here. In an effort to lift my spirits, I struck a martial arts pose, imitating the posture of David Carradine on Hua Chi's poster. *I'm an adventurer,* I told myself. *He only plays one on TV.*

I checked the compass again and began hiking west under cover of trees and shadows as I set out on the last leg of my journey, overland toward the promised Taishan Forest in the foothills of Mount Tai.

Three days later, tired and hungry, having finished most of my remaining food, I passed near Heihe. Against my better judgment, I felt an urge to enter the city and walk through crowds of people instead of endless trees. But Hua Chi's advice held me back. I had to avoid the authorities. What had that bearded driver asked me on the ride to Los Angeles? Now I really *was* sticking it to the man. Buoyed by that thought, I continued onward, recalling a proverb I'd read: "When on a long trek, it's okay to quit whenever you like, as long as your feet keep moving."

That evening sheer exhaustion turned the ground to a featherbed, and I slept like the dead. Near dawn, I emerged from a strange dream of a sunlit pavilion and a woman dressed in white, until her tunic turned into a shaft of sunlight striking my closed eyes. At first I didn't know where I was. Then it came rushing back. I rose, stiff and hungry, and ate half of my remaining rations. My shrunken stomach growled for more.

After days of hiking on little food, I found that the forest itself took on a dreamlike quality. Several times a day I reached into my knapsack, taking comfort in the presence of Soc's journal, an anchor to a reality beyond my immediate destination. I shoved my own notebook to the knapsack's bottom, aware that it too was hungry—hungry for the words I had yet to write.

According to the map, I should have arrived by now.

But distance on a map and in a forest can be deceptively different. Searching for higher ground, I stepped into a clearing and saw a man pissing against a tree. Before I could move, he saw me, smiled, and asked something in Mandarin. I could only reply with a good-natured shrug.

He looked me up and down, taking in my dirty trousers and sweat-stained shirt, my knapsack and Red Army cap. Pointing to his nose, he said something that sounded like "Wu Shih." Nodding, he pointed at me.

"Dan Millman," I said, touching my own nose.

Without even attempting my name, he nodded, then beckoned for me to follow him. We soon approached a hut with a primitive water pump and cistern outside. He indicated that I could use the water to wash by splashing his face. I followed suit, wondering how badly I smelled—I hadn't washed for a few days. The water was clear and fast running. I gestured with my canteen, and Wu Shih seized it and filled it himself.

Now Wu Shih pulled at his shirt and gestured at me. I took off my shirt and splashed the cold water on my underarms and back and chest. After I'd put my shirt back on, he invited me into the hut. There I met a woman, presumably his wife, who bowed and then hurried to scoop some rice gruel into a small ceramic bowl. She added a few nuts that looked like almonds and chestnuts. Bowing again and smiling, she held out the bowl. We enjoyed a companionable silence as I ate until my stomach bulged. We laughed together at this.

Still, I felt awkward, as anyone might who must limit conversation to bows, smiles, gestures, and grunts. When I finished eating, Mrs. Wu Shih offered me a cup of tea and a piece of steamed bread. *"Ishi!"* she said, raising a bright red enamel cup. I wanted to offer them something in return so I held out some of my scant remaining store of raisins and mixed nuts. Bowing, Wu Shih graciously accepted just a few and put them into his gruel. His wife, however, waved my hand away.

Before I took my leave, I asked, "*Zai . . . uh,* forest . . . *uh, senlin na li?*" I gestured toward the trees to indicate a forest. Wu Shih just stared at me and shook his head, unable to make sense of my garbled language, or failing altogether to comprehend my meaning. "Taishan Forest?" I said in English, too loudly and with exaggerated gestures. Realizing they wouldn't know the word *forest*, I said "Taishan" again, trying to make it sound as Chinese as possible.

Their puzzled looks turned into another wave of laughter. Wu Shih waved his hands all around. Ah, they couldn't direct me to the mountain called Taishan, like the forest, because we were standing on it. I wanted to ask Wu Shih if he'd heard of a farm or school, but I had no way of doing so.

Moved by the hospitality they'd shown to a stranger from another land, I could only say the few words of Mandarin I knew—"*Xie xie!* Thank you!"—and bow as I moved away. They bowed back. I turned once again and entered the forest.

After another hour of walking and sweating, I came upon an impenetrable wall of foliage that looked like a larger version of Hua Chi's garden hedge—only it had no visible opening. Imagining myself back in Hong Kong, I positioned myself in front of what might have been the entrance to her home, closed my eyes, and stepped forward.

Entering the thicket, I found no small house beyond, but an altogether different landscape: Cedar and pine trees grew thick as grass. Twisted vines hung like huge snakes from massive trunks. Branches seemed to reach out and block my way every few steps, as if they resented my intrusion. A path appeared, then disappeared, like a flickering illusion as I pushed onward through the labyrinth.

I remembered having asked Hua Chi if there was a map of the Taishan Forest itself. She'd said, "It's not possible to map the forest because it changes. And compasses don't work there. Just travel with a clear intent."

A clear intent, I thought, trying to imagine a school, a farm, or a giant sign that read: YOU'RE HERE! As I plodded onward, pushing branches and vines out of the way, my hands sticky with tree sap, a flock of birds flew up from the underbrush, one of them just grazing my head, startling me. Moments later, I nearly walked through the gelatinous web of a hand-size spider. A few minutes later I pushed aside another hanging vine—only to realize that it was a sizeable snake as it slithered off.

In the shadow of the trees, I also encountered a scarlet parrot and a cascade of lemon-yellow cockatoos that whistled and chirped as they fluttered up into the boundless sky, soon hidden from my view by the canopy of leaves. The sunlight glimmered as solitary rays cut through the foliage overhead. The sun was descending sooner as the early autumn days grew shorter.

When I felt something move in the bush near my feet, fear slithered up my spine. I quickened my pace, hurrying up a gentle slope. That's when confusion came over me, as if I'd stumbled into a maze of mirrors. I began to wonder if I was traveling in circles. Another hour passed, or what seemed like an hour. I had no way of knowing since my watch battery had long since died.

I should turn around, I thought as I grew more disoriented and my heart pounded. *But in what direction? Which way is out?* In a rush, I burst out of a thicket and nearly fell over the edge of a sheer cliff. For a dizzying moment, I thought I was back on the rocky plateau in Nevada—that I'd never left it.

I blinked and saw my current surroundings once again—overlooking a deep gorge in a Chinese forest. I kicked a small stone. It fell toward what looked like a strong-flowing stream some forty feet below. If I could have turned back, I would have. But there was nowhere to go but forward, across this narrow gorge—a twelve-foot distance between myself and the opposite cliff. I could jump over it with a running start, but I had only a little clear space behind me. I looked slightly up and spotted a tree limb stretching out over the chasm. If I could grab the overhanging branch, I might be able to swing across to the other side. It was doable, especially for a former gymnast who had swung on many a branchlike bar.

Removing my knapsack, I swung it by the straps and hurled it to the other side, where it landed securely. Now I was committed. I closed my eyes and imagined myself making the leap to the branch, as I'd done so many times before trying a new move or before competing. Sinking back onto bent knees, I launched myself at the branch.

One of my shoes must have caught on an exposed root. The fingers of my desperate, outstretched hands brushed by the branch. I fell.

As an acrobat and springboard diver, I had deliberately flung my body in controlled falls over water—from piers, cliffs, and other objects. So the rush of wind and momentary disorientation were familiar to me—so familiar that I had time to yell "*Ohhhhh shiiiiiiiiiiiit!*" as I fell, instinctively ducking my head so I'd land on my back, with my feet and arms slapping to absorb the force of my landing in shallow water. It would hurt, but it would break the fall instead of my neck.

I felt a sharp sting as my body smashed into the water and then the muddy bottom three feet below. Struggling and sputtering, I was able to claw my way up onto the bank. In a rush of shock and adrenaline, I threw myself at the cliffside and began to climb, hand over hand, my feet scrambling for toeholds. When I slid down a few feet, it only triggered a more zealous effort, as if some reptilian part of me had taken command. Fingers bleeding, both knees skinned, my jeans and T-shirt torn and splattered with dirt, I reached the top and lay panting.

As my heartbeat began to slow, the power of complex thinking returned to me, and the brute strength that had coursed through me receded. Feeling drained, I forced myself to sit up. Only then did I realize that in my haste to climb, I'd scaled the cliff on the wrong side of the river—returning to the same place from which I'd leapt only a few minutes before.

Soon the sun would set, and I wouldn't even be able to see the branch—or my knapsack on the other side of the gorge. I'd already given my best effort and missed. Sore, tired, and wet, I couldn't make another attempt now. The slightest hesitation, a loose stone, a small slip, and I'd be back in the river, considerably the worse for wear. I might die if I tried again tonight. So I decided to find a place to sleep; I'd try again in the morning, when I was rested. It was going to be a long, cold night. No tarp. No food. No canteen.

Fighting off self-pity, intent on pushing through some bushes to find a small clearing I'd passed earlier, I thought I saw a dark, indistinct shape moving through the bramble. Had the fall or the river affected my vision? I took a step back, then froze as I identified the shape: a bear. The biggest, meanest-looking monster of a bear I'd ever seen. Or maybe it just looked that way because it was close enough for me to smell its breath. Standing, it towered over me and roared—a heart-stopping, bloodcurdling bellow.

I turned tail and ran like a crazy man, plunging through the thicket as though it were mist. I ran at full speed and leapt into thin air, and the branch seemed to swing into my outstretched hands. My body arced forward so quickly that I almost forgot to let go of the branch. Fortunately, no one was there to grade my dismount. I landed flat on my ass and bounced onto solid earth. My knapsack rested miraculously between my straddled legs. I didn't see the bear when I looked back across the gorge, but that didn't stop me from sliding onto my knees, shaking one fist, and giving a Bronx cheer before I collapsed.

As I lay there, a Sufi story ambled into my head: A ruler summoned a renowned sage to his court and said,

"Prove to me you're not another charlatan or I'll have you executed on the spot!"

Instantly the sage went into a trance. "I see, oh great king, rivers of silver and gold flowing through the heavens, on which ride dragons spitting fire. I see giant serpents, even now, crawling through the earth far below!"

The king, impressed, asked, "How is it that you can see far into the heavens and deep into the bowels of the earth?"

"Fear is all you need," he replied.

Amen to that, I thought, shaken and stirred like a cocktail. It was all I could do to crawl forward a few feet, putting a little more distance between myself and the cliff edge, before I curled up around the knapsack, cradling it tenderly, and fell into a sleep troubled by dreams of running and pursuit.

The next morning, chilled and hungry, I moved carefully down a steep incline, then ascended a gentler grade, pushing myself onward until midday, when I found the semblance of a path. *Another path leading nowhere*, I thought, dulled from hunger and fatigue. I moved my feet, one wobbling step after another, my body ravaged, my spirit shaken.

A few hours later, with the sun descending toward the rim of the mountains, the path came to an abrupt end.

SEVENTEEN

Stumbling into a clearing, I saw the shimmering stalks of a cultivated cornfield along with a red-roofed barn, reminding me of Ohio. Directly ahead and to the right, about a hundred yards away, lay a sturdy-looking two-story house. Beyond I could make out what looked like a pavilion, painted white, and a series of small dwellings—Chinese architecture in its purest form, with gracefully curving roofs that lifted my gaze to the orange sky. And there, in the shadow of the large roof's overhang, the figure of a man emerged. I was too far away to see him clearly, but he was watching me. I could feel it.

I heard dogs barking and saw two of them running toward me—not menacing but watchful, with a large pig trailing behind them. The trio approached cautiously. One of the dogs let me scratch it lightly behind the ears. The other cut in and shoved its nose into my palm. The pig gave a sniff too, and grunted before the welcoming committee headed back down the grade.

My eyes swept past a smaller house beside the large one to a fast-flowing stream running behind both structures. I saw a woman approaching. The last rays of the evening sun painted her white silk tunic shades of pink and gold. Conscious of my ragged appearance, I made a futile attempt to straighten my clothes and ran a dirty hand through my hair. The woman stopped a few feet away. She had an oval face with a large scar across her cheek—from a serious burn, I guessed—and beautiful eyes framed by jet-black hair tied in a single braid. She made a slow bow as if I were a visiting dignitary. She spoke in clipped, British-sounding English, her voice unexpectedly lower than Hua Chi's: "My name is Mei Bao. How can I help you?"

I made a belated attempt to bow, then turned to search through my pack for the letter I was to present to Master Ch'an. Unable to find it, I turned back to see her gazing at me, puzzled. After a speechless moment, I replied in a run-on sentence reminiscent of seven-year-old Bonita. "Oh, uh, my name is Dan Millman, you see I was sent here, well, not really sent, I mean I came of my own accord, but Hua Chi suggested I meet—"

"Hua Chi?" she said, now looking past me, over my

shoulder, perhaps expecting Hua Chi to appear behind me. After a pause: "Surely you didn't travel here on your own?"

I nodded, still preoccupied as I searched through my bag. "Somewhere I have a letter of—"

She pursed her lips. "I've forgotten my manners; you must be weary from your journey. Let me show you where you may rest for the night. In the morning we'll speak over tea. By then you'll have found the letter." Mei Bao spoke soothingly as though I were a small child who'd woken from a nightmare.

She led me to a small room just inside and to the left of the barn's entrance. There the smell of horse manure gave way to fresh, clean straw. Near a raised sleeping loft stood a makeshift desk and a box to store my things.

"I apologize for the condition. There's a dormitory where the students stay, but perhaps it's better if you stay here."

"Of course," I said. "After where I've slept recently, this room will do very nicely."

After she left, I unpacked, folded my dirty laundry and put it aside, and then set the samurai and the kachina doll on a small table, next to Soc's journal and my notebook.

I found the letter Hua Chi had written for Master Ch'an—it had slid behind the lining like everything else, it seemed. Setting it under the samurai, I lay back on the straw and took a deep breath, waiting for sleep. But my mind kept whirling: *Why did I risk my life to get here? Why did my unchaperoned arrival surprise Mei Bao? Will Master Ch'an accept me as a student?*

Awakened abruptly by the cry of a rooster above me, I pulled on my only clean pair of pants and the collared shirt I'd saved for this purpose, and stepped into the cool air of early October.

In the soft light of dawn, I could see the fields in orderly rows. A lone cat streaked by as the yelping dogs joined me, along with, yes, their pig pal. I'd seen several sheep grazing last evening, and I now passed a pen with several more pigs. This was indeed a farm.

I saw young people, mostly teenagers, their heads wrapped, heading into the fields; others walked toward what might have been a kitchen and dining hall adjacent to the pavilion I'd noticed last night. Netting hung down on all sides—to keep out insects, I guessed. Peering into the spacious pavilion, I saw mats made of rice straw like the Japanese tatami covering most of the wood-planked floor. It had taken devoted labor to build all this over the years.

Outside again, I let my gaze follow a stream that flowed between the rear of the big house and the pavilion.

An arched bridge connected the house to the pavilion entrance. On the other side of the house, a waterwheel lifted bamboo cups of water up to a second-floor window, where they spilled into what must have been a form of plumbing, sending gravity-fed running water down through the house. The entire area was silent and tranquil, at once distinct from and yet in harmony with the surrounding forest.

I jumped as Mei Bao touched my shoulder. "Would you please follow me, Mr. Millman—"

"Please call me Dan."

She nodded. "I hope you slept well. Master Ch'an would like to welcome you as a friend of Hua Chi's."

"We're not really old friends. In fact, she and I only met recently. . . ."

As we entered the house, I removed my boots, suddenly anxious.

Mei Bao said, "Just relax and be natural." Which naturally made me feel tense and awkward, knowing this was not an idle chat but a kind of interview.

After I stepped into guest slippers, we padded over a shining cedar floor to a sitting room, where he waited. The Master of Taishan Forest. Flowers were arranged on a table alongside bowls of water and cotton hand towels.

Dressed in a plain gray tunic, Master Ch'an was an imposing figure despite his small stature, a few inches over five feet. His black hair had grayed around the temples, and bushy eyebrows protruded over alert eyes. His face, absent of tension, gave no clue to his age.

I bowed and held out the folded letter Hua Chi had written. Mei Bao took it and handed it to Master Ch'an. He read it slowly. I watched his expression for any sign—a smile, a nod. Anything. He said a few words to Mei Bao and passed the letter back to her to read. Finally she spoke. "Thank you for bringing us this news from Hua Chi."

I waited for her to say something more, but she and Master Ch'an only stared at me appraisingly, exchanging small words in Chinese. *So that's it! Maybe every few months Hua Chi finds a gullible foreigner to deliver her mail.*

Mei Bao spoke again. "Hua Chi noted that you have an interest in practicing t'ai chi, and that you might also consent to teach acrobatics to our students. There are about twenty of us right now."

Ah, so that was her agenda, I thought. *Hua Chi sent me here not only as a mail carrier but as a possible teacher.* I was glad that the two of them couldn't hear my thoughts; at least, I was fairly certain they couldn't. With or without the journal, I hadn't come empty-handed, "begging alms of insight"—Soc did have a way with words when he wasn't racked by fever. "I'd be happy to help however I can," I said out loud.

Mei Bao translated my few words for Ch'an, then excused herself to prepare tea.

The master and I sat in silence as we waited for her return. Catching a sidelong glance, I noticed how his prominent cheekbones added a toughness to his wiry appearance. He projected vitality and strength.

Mei Bao returned with fragrant, steaming bowls of rice and stir-fried vegetables. I waited for Master Ch'an and Mei Bao to begin. They were apparently waiting for me. Finally Mei Bao said, "Please, enjoy your meal. After this, you'll eat in the dining hall with the students each morning following work in the fields."

As we ate, she told me of the daily routine: "For your time here, you'll rise with the rooster—"

"That shouldn't be a problem," I said, remembering my earlier wake-up call.

She laughed, then tried and apparently failed to translate the joke for Master Ch'an—if his expression was any indicator. Still smiling, she continued: "You'll work in the fields or kitchen before the main meal in the dining hall. You'll hear a bell. After that, you'll have two hours of rest and open time before afternoon training—"

Master Ch'an said something to her. She nodded, and

added, "You'll have the opportunity to practice t'ai chi for two hours, and after a short break you can teach acrobatics for the next two hours. Normally the martial arts take up the whole afternoon, but while you're here, it seems a good opportunity for the students to develop new skills of agility and balance."

I nodded, considering this new responsibility. People often assume that any skilled athlete, artist, or musician can also teach. But I'd learned that teaching is itself an art, one that requires practice. In my early teens I'd helped my friends at a trampoline center figure out how to learn or improve various somersaults. Later I offered suggestions to my college teammates and taught at a few summer gymnastics camps and clinics. My communication skills improved while coaching and teaching beginning gymnastics at Stanford and more recently at Oberlin. But I'd never before had (or wanted) the challenge of teaching young men and women tempered in the kiln of a different culture, who didn't speak my language while I couldn't speak theirs.

Our meal complete—and my stomach, as usual, still growling for more—we sipped a bitter, energizing tea. When Mei Bao stood, I started to get up as well, assuming that my meeting with Ch'an had concluded, but she checked me with a gesture.

"There's one thing more," Mei Bao added. "Just a small

test." She reached into a silver box and took out a straight pin. After she pushed the point of the pin down into the wood so that it stood upright, she turned to me. "Master Ch'an asks that you send the pin into the table."

She sat back down and waited.

I swallowed.

EIGHTEEN

The task reminded me of one of Papa Joe's riddles. I recalled the response of Alexander the Great when he confronted the tangled Gordian knot securing a closed gate that blocked his way. He was challenged to untangle the knot. A man of action, he drew his sword and sliced through it.

So, without hesitation, I slammed my palm straight down onto the pinhead with full force and concentration. My hand made a resounding *thud* as it connected with the table surface. To my surprise, the only pain I felt resulted from slapping my palm onto the table. I lifted my hand to see what had happened to the pin. It lay on the table, bent in two.

Master Ch'an nodded, his face expressionless.

Seeing my crestfallen expression at failing to drive the

pin into the table, Mei Bao reassured me. "Yours was a proper response. Your aim was true, and your commitment clear. If you had held back, the pin might have cut your skin, but the pin, like other obstacles that appear on your path, gave way to the force of your intention. You focused on the goal, not on the obstacle. This is how we face our lives."

With that, she stood, and so did I. I bowed to Master Ch'an once more. My last impression, as I left the house, was of the flowing back of Mei Bao's tunic as she disappeared through a doorway, passing quietly through a curtain of beads.

The next morning before I began the work detail, Mei Bao showed me around the farm. As we skirted the edge of the trees, she cautioned me about returning to the forest.

"It's too easy to become lost," she said.

"Do students sometimes get lost?"

"From time to time," she said seriously. "Nearly always we can find them again."

She took me out into the fields and showed me where I could get gloves.

"Just imitate what the others are doing, whether planting potatoes or practicing t'ai chi," she advised. "Please take pride in all that you do. Everything matters. We strive to remain self-sufficient and self-reliant here. Do you understand?"

I nodded, having grasped her meaning and more. On this farm I found a different China from the one I'd expected, and a revolution more profound than Mao's.

When Mei Bao departed, I pulled on the work gloves and headed out into the fields, ready to make the daily routines of the farm and school my own. At least for the next month or so.

An hour into the work of bending, hoeing, and planting, I realized how much brute labor was required to keep a farm running. As I stopped to stretch for a few moments, I noticed a muscular man about my age. He wore a long-sleeved gray cotton shirt like the others, but he was more solidly built, with a barrel chest—more wrestler than martial artist. All the younger workers had towels wrapped around their heads and wore rubber boots. I was afraid that I stood out rather comically in my hiking boots and my red star cap, but the others seemed intent on their tasks. I did my best to follow their example despite blisters.

After the work detail, and before the midday meal, I washed my face and hands in the stream alongside my companions. They stole furtive looks at me, the newcomer, a foreigner.

The small dining hall was quieter than I might have expected. The young people—mostly in their teens but a few in their twenties—spoke in whispers. When I sat down with my food near the center of the long table, everyone near me stopped speaking and cast shy glances in my direction, too polite to stare.

On impulse, drawing on the persona of my college days, I put my bowl down dramatically, stood, and then pressed up to a handstand on the table. Upside-down, seeing no one behind me, I did a snap down to my feet followed by a back handspring into a somersault. Then, as if nothing had happened, I strolled back to my table, sat down, and continued eating.

After a moment of dead silence, the room erupted with shrieks, laughter, and boisterous comments. The students near me bowed and smiled. A moment before, I had been the Foreign Stranger; now I was the Acrobat.

During the two-hour rest period, I busied myself washing pants, shirts, socks, and underwear behind the main house. While my clothing dried in the sun, draped over low branches, I returned to my nook, as I'd begun to think of it. Too tired from unaccustomed labor to think about studying Soc's notes, I slept until it was time for t'ai chi practice.

As the afternoon sun began its descent from the top of the hazy blue sky, dipping in the direction of Mongolia far to the west, I stepped into the white pavilion, where young field-workers had transformed into martial artists. All were dressed in identical blue pants and tops, so I stood out like a sore American. Which I was, after the morning work shift.

Mei Bao appeared by my side. "Master Ch'an would like you to observe for the next few days until the routine is familiar to you."

Disappointed but also relieved, I crouched down in a corner and watched the students warm up. They moved and stretched in unison while singing a rhythmic song, which Mei Bao, in passing, explained was a way to unify the group in breathing and movement.

After the warm-up, they all sat still with their eyes closed for a few minutes of deep, slow breathing, which, Mei Bao told me later, included a visualization of what they wanted to accomplish. They rose in unison and began the t'ai chi form. I noticed that Master Ch'an observed the students with a relaxed attentiveness. He stayed in the front of the room, while Mei Bao wandered among the students, occasionally returning to speak with Ch'an.

Just after class, Mei Bao told me a little of the history of t'ai chi to put my training into context: "The traditional practice of t'ai chi comes from the Chen Village, originally located near the Shaolin Temple area of Zhengzhou. Yang Luchan, a servant boy in the Chen household, was the first person outside the Chen family to learn this style. It's said that he mastered it so thoroughly that he eventually traveled to the capital of Peking, now called Beijing, and defeated so many Imperial Guards that he became known as Invincible Yang. He eventually created a Yang family dynasty.

"Legend has it that Yang Luchan taught a superficial method to the public of his time, reserving a secret indoor Yang style for his descendants and closest disciples. As it happens, Hua Chi trained with a student of this indoor style well after the collapse of the Qing dynasty. This *sifu*, or teacher, was quite old when Hua Chi met him, and he desired to pass on its methods to her, a devoted practitioner."

Turning back to me, Mei Bao said, "You'll first need to learn the precise set of one hundred and eight movements until you can embody and demonstrate six essential principles: relaxation, upright torso, separate weighting on each leg, fair lady's hand, turning at the waist, with arms and torso working in unison. At first the form is primary, and remains the foundation of internal training—opening the body and nervous system to gather energy from heaven and earth, letting it surge along the energy meridians. This improves health and also power. That's why this practice, which appears merely dancelike to the casual eye, is called t'ai chi chuan, or grand ultimate fist."

Over the coming days, I adapted to the routines and rhythms of the farm. After the evening meal, I returned to my quarters to study the journal and began to make preliminary notes in my notebook.

Just after breakfast one morning, I finally had the chance to talk more with Mei Bao. Curious about my fellow workers and students, I asked, "Where did all these young people come from? And how did they find their way here?"

"Hua Chi has many contacts, including several orphanages," she explained. "She was able to hand-select children with few prospects of adoption but with strong energy, and invite them to the farm. This isn't strictly legal, but the authorities' single-minded focus on 'revolutionary leaps' has left them with little attention to give to what happens to a few stray orphans. As you've seen, the students are grateful to be here and to work in exchange for their subsistence and t'ai chi training. Anyone who chooses to leave—and eventually most of them do leave—will have skills to serve in farming or teaching t'ai chi. Or perhaps, with your help, they can perform or even teach acrobatics."

I doubted I'd be around long enough to learn or teach much, but I left that unsaid. Instead I asked, "Have any students chosen to leave early?"

Mei Bao hesitated before speaking. "Not everyone is temperamentally suited for the life here. A few years ago, one young woman elected to return to her home city of Guangzhou. I accompanied her to Taishan Village, and we were able to arrange her passage back. And . . . just before your arrival, one of the young men, Chang Li, ran off. I hope he found his way out of the forest."

"I hope so too," I said, thinking about the bear and my own difficult journey.

Changing the subject, I asked, "Did Hua Chi's letter to Master Ch'an relate anything about my travels?" Mei Bao looked puzzled, so I told her a little about my professional purpose and—skipping over my recent adventures—shared a little about Socrates and my search for a hidden school.

"You think *this* might be the school your teacher meant?" she asked, not sounding convinced.

"I really don't know," I said. "But here I am. And while I'm here, it's likely that my mentor would encourage me to study directly with the Master of Taishan Forest. Does Master Ch'an ever take on private students?"

I thought I saw Mei Bao's lips curve upward in a smile, but it disappeared quickly. "Not likely," she answered, standing up to leave. "But I believe he'll appreciate your interest. In the meantime, you'll have to settle for whatever suggestions I can offer—and your fellow students, of course."

The following day I was invited to participate in the afternoon t'ai chi session. I knew the Buddhist saying "Comparison is a form of suffering," but I compared anyway, perhaps naturally given the stark contrast between my beginner's struggles and the graceful movements of the advanced students. Mei Bao translated Master Ch'an's reminder to focus on the proper positions and movement until I was ready for internal training. *Which might be never at my current rate of progress*, I thought.

Later, when Mei Bao asked for a show of hands from those who wished to train with me in acrobatics during the second afternoon session, every hand shot up. From one moment to the next, I went from bumbling student of t'ai chi to "distinguished teacher of acrobatics," in the words of Master Ch'an.

As it turned out, teaching here was easier and more fun than I'd thought it would be. Mei Bao was always on hand, and the students were orderly and attentive. I spoke, she translated; I demonstrated, they imitated. Meanwhile, Master Ch'an sat quietly, observing it all. Best of all, Mei Bao changed into her white tunic and joined in as my student!

She and the other students loved trying new moves involving balance, rolls, cartwheels, and, soon, basic tumbling. Unlike the stable routines of t'ai chi, the possibilities of acrobatic maneuvers were endless.

"Poetry and calligraphy are refinements of writing," I said through my translator, "and singing is a refinement of speaking. Similarly, the acrobat refines everyday movement, expanding the boundaries of physical agility and balance."

I noticed the barrel-chested fellow about my age watching me and listening intently. Later, as I finished demonstrating a move, our eyes met. He covered his fist with his other hand in the traditional martial arts bow.

Just after practice, he placed his hand on my shoulder and, with a gesture, beckoned me to walk back with him to the meal. He pounded his chest with enthusiasm and said, "Chun Han!" I also pounded my chest like Tarzan as I said my name. He pounded his chest again, and gave a short, hoarse bark, a peculiar laughter I'd hear many more times.

He and I entered the dining hall together and sat down to our main meal for the day. After that, despite knowing only a few words of each other's language, we worked together and often ate meals side by side. The other students, mostly younger, viewed Chun Han as a kind of big brother. Laid-back even in the midst of farmwork, he seemed to radiate good cheer.

One morning I wandered behind the main house and saw Chun Han doing handstand push-ups on a log, his face a mask of determination. When he caught sight of me, he quickly stopped, smiling broadly as he climbed to his feet. I invited him to do another handstand and he did so, followed by a standing back somersault. I chose him as my assistant and soon discovered that he had a gift for spotting and assisting other students through their initial work with somersaults. He pointed out two other students who also had a little acrobatic experience, and they joined in demonstrating and helping the others.

I've often wondered whether some people possess more innate energy than others, whether it's a genetic trait or luck of the draw. Whatever it was, Chun Han had it. His vitality and high spirits inspired and sometimes frustrated me. I once asked him, with Mei Bao as an interpreter, why he smiled so much. He barked and said something back to her in Mandarin, which she interpreted with a smile: "Just a bad habit."

The daily routines brought incremental progress measured in crop growth, harvested stores, t'ai chi refinements, and, now, tumbling skills. On Sundays we worked a shorter shift and spent the rest of the day on special repairs, odd jobs, and mending clothing.

Mei Bao would occasionally leave the farm—to find medicinal herbs for Master Ch'an or any students who might be ill, she explained. She also went into the village once a month—"to pick up a few essential supplies and to overhear 'footpath news,' passed as gossip, about the larger political situation," she told me. "So far, we've been spared any turmoil."

Here on this hidden farm, the world of politics seemed far away.

A few days later, on a crisp autumn day, Chun Han

gestured that I should join him on a walk into the forest near the main pavilion. He led me through a stand of trees. I waited while he moved a tangle of tied-together branches to reveal a hidden path past a small temple in the woods. Fifty yards beyond that, we arrived at the crystal-blue surface of a small lake, which reminded me of Walden Pond in Massachusetts, and the peace and inspiration Henry David Thoreau had found there.

We walked slowly together around its shore, shadowed by limbs reaching out over the water. We ducked under low-hanging branches, which dropped a carpet of leaves at our feet. Although we walked in silence, I understood an unspoken message—that by sharing with me this place he clearly loved, Chun Han deepened an empathy and friendship that transcended differences in language or culture.

Meanwhile, as I pursued my teaching duties, I continued to refine the way I offered guidance so that my students could truly make use of it. When I'd coached elite gymnasts, I often gave lengthy explanations about technique until a U.S. Olympian on my team, who'd trained for a year in Japan, quipped: "I've noticed that a Japanese coach will tell you one thing and have you practice it a hundred times. An American coach will tell you a hundred things and have you practice them once." My memory of this witty exaggeration guided me toward an economy of speech so that Mei Bao wouldn't have to spend her own practice time translating my words. Fortunately, once I'd helped my students build a foundation of proper basic movements, their learning took on its own momentum. There's a saying in the martial arts, "Learn one day, teach one day," which they did naturally, each playing the role of student and teacher for one another.

I had not at all forgotten my primary goal here—to translate and flesh out the notes and outline from Soc's journal in my own notebook, page by page. It weighed on me more each day, until I knew I had to begin. *Soon*, I told myself. *Very soon*.

After class a few days later, I decided to share a larger message with the students. After reminding them that they must not only dedicate their lives to their training but dedicate their training to their lives—and how acrobatic practice develops not only physical agility but a flexible state of mind—I taught them a simple warm-up song in English, which Mei Bao translated so they understood the meaning of each phrase. After that, before each practice began, we would sing "Row, Row, Row Your Boat."

"Many children learn this song in my country," I said, "but few people understand its deeper truths. These truths apply, as you'll see, not only to acrobatics or t'ai chi training but to all of life. The words 'Row, row, row your boat' remind us to build our lives on a foundation of action and effort, not on positive thoughts or feelings. Thinking about doing something is the same as not doing it. Our lives are shaped by what we actually do—by rowing our boat. Only effort over time brings results in training and in everyday life."

One of the students volunteered a Chinese proverb, shyly at first and then with growing enthusiasm: "With enough time and patience, one can level a mountain with a spoon!"

"Exactly!" I said, hearing myself echo Papa Joe's *¡Exactamente!*

"The next four words, 'gently down the stream,' advise us to avoid unnecessary tension, to row with the flow of the Tao, the natural tides and currents of life—"

"What we Chinese call *wu wei*, or nonresistance," Mei Bao added.

"And 'merrily, merrily, merrily, merrily' is a repeated reminder to live with a lighthearted spirit, to take ourselves less seriously, and to solve the problems of daily life with the same fun-loving attitude you bring to learning acrobatics." With that, I dove into a handstand and clapped my feet together. The students followed enthusiastically. I heard Chun Han's hoarse bark from the back of the group.

"Finally, consider the last line of the song: 'Life is but a dream.' Please discuss its meaning with one another during the evening meal."

Before they departed, I asked my students to gather around me, and I reminded them of a Taoist folktale about

Joshu, a worker in China who had to row his small boat up and across the Fen each day to reach his work. "In the morning," I said, warming to the tale, "Joshu had to row against the current, but the trip home was far easier. One morning, as he pulled his oars, making his way upstream, he felt a sudden jolt as the craft of another boatman collided with his rowboat. Joshu shook his fist at the careless boatman, yelling, 'Watch where you're going!' It took him many minutes to calm down as he thought about how people should pay better attention. No sooner had his anger subsided than he felt *another* jolt as a different craft struck his boat. He couldn't believe it! Now fully enraged, he turned to berate another idiot. But his words fell away and his anger vanished as he saw an empty boat that must have pulled loose from its moorings and drifted downstream.

"So what do you think this story means?" I asked as a smiling Mei Bao translated.

The students discussed the story among themselves before one of them spoke. Mei Bao told me, "Hai Liang says we must treat everyone like an empty boat."

I smiled and nodded with approval, which seemed to make the students as proud as they had made me.

Later, as I watched their animated conversation in the dining hall, Mei Bao told me, "They're earnestly discussing how life might be a wonderful dream."

NINETEEN

Something about teaching these dedicated students made it easier for me to finally return to the journal. As I continued to study Soc's notes and to find the thread of a theme, I started to believe, for the first time, that I might have something beyond acrobatics and children's songs to share. Completing this journal would be a beginning. In the future I might write something more.

I saw an image of Soc's smiling face. For a moment, I actually felt his presence.

That night, as I prepared to write in earnest, a stillness fell upon the farm. When I went outside the next morning, I discovered that snow had blanketed the fields and sharply angled rooftops. Winter had arrived early. Two months had already passed, and it now appeared likely that

Hua Chi—if or when she came to fetch me—wouldn't arrive until spring.

I shared my concerns with Mei Bao, but she could only shrug. Neither she nor Master Ch'an had the means to get an American safely back to Hong Kong. I drew some small comfort from the knowledge that if Hua Chi did arrive after the spring thaw, I'd still have time for my Japan visit since I didn't have to return to Ohio until June.

The next evening I ate quickly, excused myself, and returned to the barn. Feeling my way to the small table, I retrieved my small box of matches. The room glowed as a match burst into flame. I carefully lit the oil lamp, then opened the journal. I transcribed the first short paragraph exactly as Soc had written it, most likely before the fever overcame him. He began:

> *After a long preparation, the whole of life comes into view. Not only daily life, but a larger arena from which all wisdom springs, founded on an appreciation for paradox, humor, and change.*

Paradox, humor, and change: I recalled these three words printed on an unusual business card Socrates had given me years before, which I still carried in my wallet. On several occasions I'd been tempted to use the card to call him as he'd said I might, promising to appear "in some form" to offer guidance. *Maybe now in the form of Master*

Ch'an, I thought. I opened my wallet and drew out the card; now dog-eared and ordinary-looking, it no longer glowed. (Had it ever? I was no longer certain.) I slid it back into my wallet as a reminder of our time together, and turned back to Soc's notes and my writing.

I thought about related fragments of text from parts of the journal Soc must have written after the fever took hold:

> *Change: death of one thing, birth of another. Humor: true humor beyond jokes or laughter. Relaxed acceptance, nonserious . . . life a game. Paradox: gateway to wisdom . . . apparent contradictions, both true. . . Buddhist five truths . . . Dickens's best of times . . . Nasruddin, you're right . . . four key areas . . . must realize, reconcile.*

Socrates had wanted to elaborate on these ideas. *What would Soc have written in a more complete draft?* I wondered. *Can I grasp his meaning?* My mind went as blank as the page in front of me.

Then I wondered, *What if I wanted to share Soc's ideas with my students? How would I express them?* With these questions floating in the air, I began to read and then to write, circling back to scratch out a sentence in my notebook, determined to make my way forward through his jungle of notes.

When I felt I had done all I could at the time, I went over the words again and again, cutting here, adding there, as the work took on a momentum of its own and I lost myself in it.

Finally, late in the night, I read over what I had written. Although Soc's business card listed the three words in the order of paradox, then humor, then change, I chose to save paradox for last, so I began with change:

> Life is a sea that brings waves of change, welcome or not. As the warrior-emperor Marcus Aurelius wrote, "Time is a river of passing events. No sooner is one thing brought to sight than it's swept away, and another takes its place, and this too will be swept away." The Buddha, leaving behind both his protected childhood and ascetic renunciation, and having attained illumination, observed, "Everything that begins also ends. Make peace with this and all will be well."

> Humor, in its highest sense, transcends the momentary tension release of laughter, and expands into a profound sense of ease and a relaxed approach to life's occasional challenges, large or small. When you view your

world through this lens of transcendent humor, as if from a distant peak, you discover that life is a game you can play as if it matters—with a peaceful heart and a warrior's spirit. You can remain engaged with the world but also rise above it, looking beyond your personal dramas.

Paradox is any self-contradictory proposition that, when investigated, may prove to be well-founded or true. Once understood, it opens the gateway to higher wisdom. But how can contradictory principles both be true?

As the Buddhist Riddle of Five Truths puts it: "It is right. It is wrong. It is both right and wrong. It is neither right nor wrong. All exist simultaneously."

Charles Dickens expressed the paradox of his era, equally true today, when he wrote, "It was the best of times, it was the worst of times, it was the age of wisdom, it was the age of foolishness," going on to describe that time as one of belief and incredulity, light and darkness, hope and despair.

Two opposing statements can each be true depending on the observer: it's true that spiders are merciless killers from the viewpoint of tiny insects caught in their webs—but for most humans, nearly all spiders are harmless creatures.

A story of the Sufi sage Mullah Nasruddin expresses the nature of paradox when he's asked to arbitrate between two men with opposing views. Hearing the first man, he remarks, "You're right." When he hears the second man, he also says, "You're right." When a bystander points out, "They can't both be right," the mullah scratches his head and says, "You're right."

Let's go deeper and consider four central sets of paradoxical truths:

* Time is real. It moves from past to present to future.
* There is no time, no past, no future—only the eternal present.

* You possess free will and can thus take responsibility for your choices.
* Free will is an illusion—your choices are influenced, even predetermined, by all that preceded them.

* You are, or possess, a separate inner self existing within a body.
* No separation exists—you are a part of the same Consciousness shining through billions of eyes.

* Death is an inevitable reality you'll meet at the end of life.
* The death of the inner self is an illusion. Life is eternal.

Must you choose one assertion and reject the other? Or is there a way to meaningfully resolve and even reconcile such apparent contradictions? All that follows addresses this question.

I sat back, intoxicated and exhausted from my mental labors. *Are these words mine or his?* I wondered. Back in that service station years ago, Socrates had pointed to a few of these contradictory truths. It seemed to me even now, in the light of my everyday reality, that only the first statement of each pair was undeniably true—that time passes, that free choice exists, that we are (or have) an inner self, and that we each die.

With that thought, I blew out the lamp and lay down for the night, breathing in the rich barn aromas of straw and earth, which pervaded the air like Chinese incense.

I spent the bulk of the next morning helping to remove stones from a new plot of land. I saw Master Ch'an in the distance, looking in my direction. *I can't just ask him to tutor me personally*, I thought, *but if he sees how hard I'm working and how sincere I am . . .* I took large steps, grunted, and occasionally wiped my brow to announce my efforts. I glanced back at Master Ch'an in time to see him turn his back and enter his house.

Later that morning, Chun Han pushed one of the large stones we'd gathered that morning into my arms and gestured for me to follow. He led me to the stream, where we placed my stone and the one he'd carried deep in the water. Continuing this process through the long morning, stone by heavy stone, we gradually constructed a dam several feet high with an opening at the top, resulting in a waterfall. Both of us were covered in sweat despite the chill air. Fatigued from the labor, I felt irritated at Chun Han's smiles and cheery manner until the words from the song arose from the recesses of my mind: "Gently down the stream . . ."

When I returned to the barn, I found winter clothes waiting for me—a new pair of wool pants and a thick cotton jacket. At least someone appreciated my work, even if not Master Ch'an.

The next morning, I saw Mei Bao head into the forest, accompanied by a student.

That afternoon, since Mei Bao still hadn't returned, Master Ch'an stood alone, watching us all as we moved through the t'ai chi forms. I could feel my practice improving. Now more attuned to internal energy flow, I felt a warmth in my fingertips, a sign that my joints and sinews were opening. It wasn't, I realized, an esoteric achievement, but a natural result of mindful practice and repeated reminders to relax. As Master Ch'an watched, I allowed the movement to unfold without an ounce more effort than necessary. As usual, he spoke little, and never to me.

When Mei Bao returned just before acrobatics practice, I asked about her trip. "Gathering herbs," she said. "This way each student learns where to find them." I hoped she'd ask me to come along one of these days but understood that the Chinese students had priority.

The exuberant tumbling routines later in the afternoon served as a perfect complement to the internalized slow-motion t'ai chi practice. Making the most of this contrast, I tried to vary our lively workouts for fun. So, near the end of practice, with Mei Bao translating, I proposed a race between Chun Han and another of the older students down a long row of mats. They would begin the race at the same moment. The other student's task was simply to run as fast as he could, parallel to the length of the tumbling strip, to the other end of the room. Chun Han would sprint a few feet forward and do a roundoff to turn his body around, followed immediately by a series of backward handsprings to propel him rapidly down the tumbling area.

I posed the question: "Who will win the race?" The students excitedly gathered to watch. They cheered loudly when Chun Han won the race by about a second. They all wanted to take turns trying similar races—I didn't need Mei Bao to point out to them how their tumbling would soon become lighter and faster.

TWENTY

Even as I moved through the routines of farmwork, martial arts, and acrobatics, I couldn't stop ruminating on the paradoxes that formed the heart of what Socrates had intended to express in the journal. At first these paradoxes made me uncomfortable. It wasn't until I'd become completely absorbed in watching my students' flight through space that an idea—the first glimmer of something like understanding—took shape. I returned to my desk that evening, knowing what I wanted to write, what I had to write, even before I opened my notebook. I wrote and revised, wrote and revised, into the early-morning hours.

I put the journal aside and waited until the next morning to discover where my pen, with Soc's guidance, had taken me—to read what I had somehow written.

There's a way to reconcile the four central paradoxes of life, and to embrace the truth of each. In order to make this leap, consider that all of these paradoxes revolve around a so-called self that is born and dies. In everyday life, you identify with an "I" that seems to be rooted somewhere inside your head. But what if this sense of an inner self is an illusion? What might lie on the other side of such a discovery? To better understand, let's explore another illusion that seems as true as your individual identity.

In this moment, you sit or stand on what appears to be, what feels like, a solid object, something real. When you extend a hand to shake, or to reach for a loved one, or simply to open a door to the next room, you feel as if you're making physical contact. But so-called solid matter, we now know, is made from molecules, composed of atoms, which consist mostly of empty space. No object truly touches any other, not in the popular sense. Rather, fields of energy interact with one another, as in the t'ai chi exercise of push hands, where partners alternately assert and receive, playing with energy in motion.

I found myself poking the desktop, noticing how real and solid it seemed. But thinking about mostly empty space and energy fields drew me back into the mystery and magic I'd experienced with Socrates years before. I continued reading.

You can imagine the atomic level, but you can't truly navigate there. Yet something changes, both profoundly and subtly, when you consider how reality may differ from what you sense in ordinary awareness. A gap opens up. And if you gaze into that gap, that small tear in the lining of the universe, a new vision becomes possible.

In ancient India, a forest wanderer encountered the Buddha without recognizing him. "Are you a wizard?" he asked. The Buddha smiled and shook his head. "Surely you're a king or a great warrior!" Again the Buddha said no. "Then what is it that makes you different from anyone I've ever met?" asked the wanderer. The Buddha turned to him.

When their eyes met and held, the Buddha said, "I am awake."

Such an awakening is a primary aim of most spiritual paths. Also referred to as realization, union, kensho, samadhi, satori, fana, enlightenment, and liberation, it involves seeing through and beyond the so-called inner self. Why do so many of us yearn for this awakening? Perhaps because we fear death in all its incarnations—the death of those we love, the death of hope, the death of meaning, the death of the body, the death of the self.

But before you can awaken, you need to notice that you're in some sense asleep—dreaming within a consensual reality until you taste the transcendent. Even a glimpse can change lives. You need not realize absolute enlightenment to find relief. Even in the midst of an ordinary day, a subtle shift in awareness can bridge the temporal and the transcendent, momentarily liberating you from the fear of death and revealing the gateway to eternal life.

Practicing enlightenment before enlightenment, I thought. *What a novel idea. Or is it? What has Socrates been trying to tell me all this time? And how,* exactly, *can seeing through this separate, inner self—a kind of death in itself—offer an escape from death and a doorway to eternal life?* Another paradox, another riddle.

TWENTY-ONE

By early February, we were doing most of our labor indoors, focusing on repairs and maintenance work, and making sure the animals were well tended. We stored and dried more food and prepared outdoor ice chests to be left in the cold earth.

Soon the frozen winds were sweeping in across the unprotected North China Plain. Dry, dusty winter monsoons blew in from Mongolia and the distant Gobi Desert. There were days that felt colder, much colder, than the biting Ohio winter. At night, a small wood-burning stove kept us warm from the wind but could do nothing about the dust that settled over everything.

In our t'ai chi sessions, we intensified push-hands practice, working together in pairs as partners alternated between active and receptive roles, pushing and yielding, shifting weight, as we had learned, from fullness to emptiness. The more relaxed of the pair easily uprooted the other, sending the partner careening backward to be caught by another student. I had little previous experience with push hands, and was forced to take one or several steps backward many times when my partner detected a point of tension. It was as frustrating as anything I'd ever practiced, and left me feeling inept day after day.

For some time now, I'd also found the writing challenging. Over the first few sessions, I'd produced pages with what, in retrospect, seemed like ease. Now I sometimes spent an entire evening on one or two sentences.

Even as I found both t'ai chi and writing frustrating, in training I always had the example of the other students to push me onward, not to mention Chun Han's good-natured encouragement. Once, as he and I stretched each other's limbs, I even caught a rare smile of approval from Master Ch'an. I had no time to enjoy the moment, due to a pain in the muscles of my right thigh, which had never fully recovered from my motorcycle crash years before.

Meanwhile, the winds rarely abated. When their frigid whispers turned to howls and the dust and the snow blew in flurries, the farm lost a measure of its charm. In quiet moments, I closed my eyes and retreated into memories of lying in the warm sand on a California beach.

One morning I woke up so stiff that I had to run in

place to thaw out. Later Chun Han and I continued our custom of sharing a pot of tea and trading a few new words in English and Mandarin. I found it challenging to remember that each word in Mandarin had a different meaning depending on which of four tones was used. Chun Han found it equally challenging to master English pronunciation, such as when he asked me if I wanted a "snake" when he meant "snack." But with the help of funny stick figures we drew to convey ideas, we managed to understand each other most of the time.

As my t'ai chi training continued and I began to execute the forms with more precision and deeper levels of relaxation, I occasionally experienced what I called "zaps," energy pulses flowing through me. As grosser layers of tension fell away, I became aware of the stuck places where subtle tensions remained. Gradually my push-hands practice showed signs of improvement. But as soon as I thought I'd mastered something, no matter how small, someone would send me flying.

Would I have made any real progress by the time Hua Chi appeared? *If only I could spend just a little time working one-on-one with Master Ch'an!* But that didn't seem too likely. Even the most advanced students trained only with one another. I felt grateful that Mei Bao, at least, often wandered by, always willing to translate a question or to explain a subtle point.

After dinner one evening, in a moment of ill humor, I asked her how Master Ch'an avoided turning the place into a sort of cult. "After all," I declared, "it's an isolated farm under the sole authority of a central, charismatic figure. . . ."

Mei Bao's eyebrows twitched. She said she would ask Master Ch'an this question.

The next day she returned with an answer. With a wave of her arm, she pointed to the barn, the fields, the small house, and the pavilion. "Perhaps in one sense we *are* like a cult. But does it seem like an evil one? Are the students hypnotized? Are they sickly or unhappy or exploited? Or are they being served even as they serve? Look with your eyes. Feel with your heart. And you might as well think with your brain."

What she said next showed unexpected candor: "If you look beyond this farm to the whole of China, you'll find millions of people living under the absolute authority of the 'great helmsman,' whose words everyone must memorize and recite aloud. Absolute decrees and pronouncements, manipulation and propaganda. Brothers have turned against brothers, children against parents, parents against each other, all trying to outdo one another in their enthusiastic shows of zeal and unquestioning support, all seeking the approval of the 'supreme leader.' That's where you'll find your cult, where God is the state, and the state is one man, served by those who fall into line or are purged." She stopped abruptly; I wasn't sure she'd intended to speak so freely or forcefully. "Master Ch'an and I believe that our people will move beyond this period in our history."

"Are those Master Ch'an's words or your own?" I asked, speaking more bluntly than I'd intended.

"It doesn't matter whose words express this idea," she said deliberately. "It remains true."

These final words echoed in my mind as I returned to the barn after the meal. Before I continued writing, I read over the few pages I'd managed to produce over the last few weeks:

> As an infant, were you aware of an inner self? Or was this sense of identity learned as a social convention? In the first month or two after birth, pure awareness existed in a dreamlike state of undifferentiated oneness, swimming in a soup of sensations that made no sense, had no meaning. But gradually, during the first year of your life, this new sense of "you" began to understand what your parents meant when they pointed to your body and called you by a name.

Every child who toddles away from this state of expansive awareness learns to organize perceptions around a focal point called I. Only later, as an adult, can you discover the pathway back to the garden of innocence while retaining the wisdom of experience. You can even learn to cross back and forth between the two worlds. Spiritual masters, artists, gardeners, doctors, manicurists, students, or panhandlers may, in any moment, and for whatever reason, seek out something they cannot name—the desire for a higher vantage point from which to grasp the larger truth and possibility of their own lives.

At first I felt my doubts recede. But what had I achieved in writing this translation of Soc's ideas? Socrates might appreciate my words, but what would another reader make of them? *Can a person truly cross a bridge between worlds from one moment to the next?* I turned back a few pages to reread what I'd written.

You need not realize absolute enlightenment to find relief. Even in the midst of an ordinary day, a subtle shift in awareness can bridge the *temporal and the transcendent, momentarily liberating you from the fear of death and revealing the gateway to eternal life.*

Even as I blended Soc's insights with my carefully chosen words, I felt tempted to dismiss such lofty notions as impractical speculation—only I couldn't bring myself to do so. Throughout the time we'd trained together, Socrates had told me things that at first seemed outlandish. But later his words came to feel more true and essential than all the lessons of my youth. These memories were so vivid that it felt as if I might find Soc's service-station office in the next room. In this state of mind, I decided to tackle one of his more difficult ideas, dealing with the question and paradox, the benefits and liabilities, of identity.

Your identity as a man, a woman, a member of a particular profession, club, tribe, or religion brings a sense of inclusion and community. But every inclusion breeds an exclusion, every self an other, and every us creates a them.

Each day you tap into empathic bonds of identity with family, friends, and lovers. You identify with characters in literature and film, enabling you to immerse yourself in story worlds, transcending the self thousands of times across a lifetime. And just as you can identify with a character in a story and know simultaneously that you're not really that character, you can discover that you also play a character in everyday life.

Realizing this reality opens a gap in the fabric of the world, enabling you to pass through. It becomes possible to live as if you have a self without being imprisoned by it. This marks the beginning of freedom and the spontaneous life, in which consistency is overrated, expectations are ignored, and self-transcendence is not only a possibility but a practice.

As the borders of the limited self—the isolated, immutable self—become permeable, transparent, the idea of death becomes flimsier, less substantial, more open to question and interpretation. What effect will this have as you consider the loss of something that might not exactly exist?

Weeks passed. I often thought about my daughter even though I knew there was no way to reach her. I thought about what kind of father I wanted to be when we were together again. In the chill of late February, after the snowdrifts had thinned, Mei Bao invited me to accompany her to Taishan Village, a half-day's hike. I filled out the postcard I'd picked up in Hong Kong, just in case.

We left the next day after dawn, moving fast, ducking under low branches, stepping over fallen logs. Mei Bao clearly wasn't worried about getting lost in the forest. At times the trail narrowed, and it was all I could do to stay on her heels.

"Why make these trips yourself?" I asked. "Can't you have someone from the town deliver what you need?"

"That wouldn't be possible," she said. "As you know, it's not easy to find us."

"I found you."

"You were meant to."

"You believe that?"

She didn't answer.

Later, when we could walk side by side again and her pace slowed, I asked her about herself, where she came from, how she'd learned English.

At first she was silent, perhaps wondering how much to share. Then she began haltingly: "I was born in Hong Kong, and my earliest memories are happy ones. When I was six years old, the tenement house where my family lived burned down. It was late at night. While everyone else slept, I sometimes crawled out of my bed and played on the floor. When the fire began, a burning beam fell directly onto my empty bed," she said, touching her scarred cheek. "The beam also shattered a window, allowing for my escape. My parents, my sisters and brothers, everyone else in the building—they were all killed. All but me. I felt unworthy, being the only survivor.

"Because there was no one left to take care of me, I roamed the streets, begging. A few people took pity on me, but in the end no one wanted a scarred girl. Eventually, by chance or destiny, I found my way to the house of Hua Chi. I didn't meet her then. I'd only found her garden, a forest of flowers, which seemed a good place to hide at night. By day, I went begging. I returned to the garden each evening to sleep in my new sanctuary.

"From my hiding place, I'd watch Hua Chi as she left the house each morning and returned later in the day. I didn't reveal myself at first, for fear she would scold me and forbid me to sleep there.

"Hua Chi later told me that she'd known of my presence from the first day. Her senses are keen. It wasn't until later that she began leaving fruit on a white napkin near my hiding place. At first I just thought she was feeding the birds. When I realized that it was meant for me, I showed myself. She returned one day and found me sitting on her front steps, waiting for her. She likes to tell this story; she always mentions how neatly I folded the napkin." Mei Bao seemed lost in her memories. Her fingers moved as though she were once again folding the napkin.

"Hua Chi took me in. She taught me how to live. She sent me to schools where I learned languages—English, French, German. I studied diligently to please my new mother.

"She also encouraged me to become proficient in several different styles of martial arts. For my health, she said, but I sensed as well that she never wanted me to be exploited again. When I was eleven, she brought me to this place. Master Ch'an has been my father ever since."

Suddenly Mei Bao's attention snapped back to the present. She turned and pointed into the shadows. "There—look." Two shining eyes and a midnight-black face dissolved as soon as I saw them.

"A leopard," she said. "One of the Guardians." After that, I glanced behind me many times as we continued on the path.

When we reached the outskirts of the village—sooner than I'd expected, given my last experience alone in the forest—Mei Bao suggested that I wait in the cover of the trees. Disappointed at first, I understood her caution and agreed. It wouldn't do for her to be seen with a foreigner.

Even from this isolated outpost, "footpath news" traveled fast and far.

I nearly forgot to give her my postcard and a little of my Chinese currency, asking if she might post it to my daughter for me. She hesitated for a few moments, and then agreed. "I'll write a few characters in Chinese at the top before handing it to the shopkeeper. He'll be less likely to notice the English writing."

I didn't have to wait too long. Mei Bao returned, carrying bolts of cotton cloth and silk as well as dried fruit. I carried most of her purchases in an improvised pack she gave me. She'd been able to post the card without problems.

On the way back, we stopped to pick some red winterberries and to gather a few sprigs of the Hong Hua herb for Master Ch'an. Mei Bao knew just where to find it, brushing away the cover of snow.

We were making good progress, following the same path we'd blazed earlier through the snow, when I heard a crashing sound nearby, like a falling tree. I looked up, horrified, to see Mei Bao falling, rolling backward to the side of the path. Standing over her, lunging toward her, was the same huge bear that had sent me hurtling over the gorge.

TWENTY-TWO

Mei Bao lay staring up as the bear raised one lethal paw. The next thing I knew, I was charging forward. I heard a ferocious yell—my own. Seemingly startled, the bear backed away. I thought I heard a moan and went to Mei Bao's aid. She'd clasped a hand over her mouth—to stifle a laugh!

"What the hell's going on? You're not hurt?"

"N-n-no, Dan." She began to giggle as her hand fell away from her mouth. "I'm fine. But you may have hurt Hong Hong's feelings. He was just playing with me."

"Hong Hong?! It has a name?"

"Why are you whispering?" She laughed even harder, unable to speak. I heard a scraping sound and turned to see Hong Hong rubbing against a tree.

"Please don't frighten him more," Mei Bao said, climbing to her feet. "He's really a very well-behaved bear. He too is a Guardian of the forest. Few of the animals are tame anymore, but Hong Hong is special to us. He often sneaks up on me, or tries to, and pushes me over. I'm so glad you didn't hurt him!" I couldn't quite believe what she was saying until she reached out to scratch the fur on the bear's neck and he settled placidly back onto all fours. "Say you're sorry, Dan; he has sensitive feelings."

Staring at his snout, I managed to say, "Hello, uh, sorry I frightened you, Hong Hong." I held out my hand, wondering if I'd get it back again. The bear sniffed it loudly, took another look at Mei Bao, grunted, and then lumbered back into the forest.

"I think he likes you," she said. "You were brave. You didn't know that he's tame. Hong Hong can make some people nervous."

"No kidding," I said, relating my first acquaintance with him.

Laughing, Mei Bao said, "You showed courage to save my life. I'm grateful." She bowed.

"Reminds me of the time I made a vicious bull run."

"Really? How did you do that?"

"It was easy. I ran away, and the bull ran after me."

She laughed again. The sun now appeared to hang just above her head. She noticed it too. "We'd better increase our pace if we're to reach the school before dusk."

Half an hour later, as we crossed down through the field, only the farm cat came out to greet us with a loud *meow*. "Could you translate that for me?" I asked.

In response, Mei Bao said, in a modest display of wit: "I could if she spoke Mandarin, but she only speaks Catonese."

That evening, too tired to write, I went directly to bed. But the next day, during the morning break and in the evening, I began working to expand upon what Socrates had to say about science and faith.

> Science and faith represent two different worldviews that express the paradox of conventional and transcendental truths—one of the body and another of the soul. If an idea can be tested, it falls within the realm of science; if not, it resides in the realm of faith. Both are worthy of respect, but let's not confuse one with the other. Science has emerged as a dominant method of exploring reality. Faith remains a source of inspiration and comfort for many. Science and technology may lead to a brighter, more peaceful future. Faith calls us to our highest ideals of love and service, and to our essential unity. At the farthest reaches of scientific exploration, we

confront mysteries bordering on faith. As faith becomes self-aware, seeing the limits of old stories, it finds new narratives resonant with humanity's evolving wisdom.

All the enduring constructs or models that anchor you to a consensual reality—including religious or metaphysical ideas about God, the soul, heaven, or reincarnation—survive because they claim to fathom and explain the mystery of life. You may accept such ideas as revealed truth or as metaphor according to your values and needs. Or you may reject them. Whether theories of science or articles of faith are true may be less important than whether they're useful. Do they bring comfort or clarity? Do they help you to see higher truths, or draw you deeper into illusion? You can choose for yourself what you hold true, but you can't decide for others.

Here on the farm, where life was so simple and practical as I worked, trained, taught, ate, and slept, it felt odd to articulate such lofty ideas about the nature and meaning of our existence. Even as I reminded my students to connect their acrobatic training with the practice of life, I wondered: *Is it all wishful thinking and philosophical speculation? Or is there something I've missed? Will this writing help me find the meaning I seek, or shall I abandon the quest altogether?*

That night I tossed and turned. When I heard the rooster's cry, I wasn't sure that I'd slept at all. That day I became so racked with doubt that I put my own journal aside for a few days and returned to Soc's notes, reading them over and over. *Looking for another sign, Dan?* I mocked myself after yet another night of troubled contemplation.

The following evening, I decided not to go to sleep, not to even get up from my desk, until I'd made a real attempt to answer my own question. I returned to the first pages I'd produced, back when the writing felt effortless. One phrase in particular jumped out at me: "life is a game you can play as if it matters." *As if* . . . I thought, and I began to write.

Even from an individual perspective, in any given moment you can experience and perceive the world from either of two levels.

From a conventional view, suitable for dealing with the stuff of everyday life, you live as if you're an individual self—what you perceive and what happens is real and matters. From a transcendent view, you find yourself less attached and more ecstatic (or unreasonably happy). You live as if both you and the world are part of an intriguing dream. Each perspective brings a different experience. As the proverb goes, "Two men looked out of prison bars. One saw mud, and the other saw stars."

You can access either state of awareness by a shift in attention. In any given moment or circumstance, you can remain fully functional in the conventional world even as you appreciate the transcendent vision sought by religious and spiritual practitioners everywhere.

I reread what I'd written and let it settle awhile before I was finally prepared to return to the four paradoxes:

From a conventional view, the following four statements are true, and supported by our everyday experience and consensual reality.

First: Time passes.

Second: You make free choices and are responsible for them.

Third: You are (or have) an inner self.

Fourth: Death is real, inevitable, and final.

From a <u>transcendent</u> view, the following four statements are true, and founded on an expansive vision reflecting the realizations and testimonies of numerous spiritual adepts, mystics, philosophers, and scientists who have glimpsed another order of reality.

First: Time is a human construct; only the eternal present exists.

Second: Your choices are predetermined by a chain of factors within and without.

Third: No separate inner self exists—only the same Consciousness (or Awareness) shining through billions of eyes.

Fourth: Death cannot exist because that one Consciousness is never born and can never die.

Be content to look on transcendent truths as you do on the stars, seeing them clearly only from time to time. To peer through the clouds and fog, take a closer look at the conventional and transcendent truths of the four paradoxes:

Time passes. * There's no time, only the eternal present.

Time is a human construct that we accept as real. The second hand moves and the minutes tick by—hours, days, years. At ten o'clock you recall what you were doing at nine o'clock. You speak of yesterday, today, and tomorrow as time moves forward, waiting for no one. Aging bodies—your own, and the bodies of those with whom you share your life—provide proof of the passing of time.

From a transcendent view, all you have is this (and this and this) present moment. All else is memory, what you call the past, and imagination, what you call the future. But the past no longer exists, and tomorrow never comes.

You sit in a boat floating down the river of time. Someone on shore sees the conventional view of a boat moving from past to present to future—even as you sit absolutely still, in the eternal present.

You are free to choose. * Every choice is determined by all that came before.

Each day you make choices, limited by circumstance. With every decision, you demonstrate your freedom to choose. You are thus responsible—to one or another degree—for your choices as well as for their moral and legal consequences. Human society works more smoothly when you accept this reality.

From a transcendent perspective, your choices and actions emerge as a natural and inevitable consequence of all the historical, genetic, and environmental forces that have shaped you. As one sage put it: Every event that has occurred, the birth of every star and every molecule, every life evolving or action taken by anyone who has ever lived, has brought you to this moment. You can choose whatever you wish—but can you choose what you will choose? Or do your apparent decisions flow from unconscious factors?

I was satisfied that I had conveyed the meaning and message that Socrates had intended, but I felt troubled by the idea that our choices are predetermined. If free will was an illusion, what about responsibility?

I thought about icons from history—great philosophers, villains, and saints. *Do they choose the paths that lead them to renown, infamy, or martyrdom? Can any of us know or choose our future? Does our will carry us forward, or does a blend of fate and fortune shape our lives?*

With such ruminations churning in my mind, I continued writing.

We are separate selves. * We are each and all part of the same Consciousness.

In any given moment, other bodies don't feel your pain, think your thoughts, or feel your emotions. Thus, you operate as an independent self. With every misunderstanding you become newly aware of your separateness.

From a transcendent perspective, "I" is a persistent illusion. Billions of bodies live everyday lives without the necessity (or existence) of an independent inner self at the controls.

<u>Death is real.</u> * <u>Life is eternal.</u>

If you have sat with a dying person or viewed a body after death, you have observed its reality. The body grows cold and soon begins to decompose. The spark of life force that once shone through that body's eyes is extinguished.

From a transcendent perspective, bodies come and go with no more effect on Consciousness than a leaf falling from a tree affects the whole. You can mourn the loss that you associate with the death of the physical body without accepting it as the only truth. In the eternal present, even as loved ones cast off the husk of separateness, they continue to inhabit you in memory and in every way they have touched you over the course of your time together.

What you refer to as "I" is not merely aware—"I" is Consciousness that is never born and never dies. With this realization, death of the physical body becomes entirely natural and acceptable. The sages took life as it came, and took death without care.

You may grasp this insight now, then you may forget, then remember. In those moments of remembering, when this transcendent truth penetrates your heart, you realize who you truly are—and you attain eternal life.

The poet Alfred, Lord Tennyson, experienced this realization early in life: "Since boyhood, by repeating my own name silently, an intense awareness of individuality came, then seemed to dissolve and fade away into boundless being, and this was not a confused state, but clear and sure, utterly beyond words, where death was an almost laughable impossibility."

I was tired from tussling with ideas, old and new, and in no condition to contemplate anything more, at least for the night. I recalled something Socrates had once told me: "There is no victory over death; there is only the realization of Who we all really are." Now I could understand his meaning. Even so, I would still grieve the deaths of friends and loved ones from a conventional state of awareness. But I was beginning to grasp that such loss was not the only truth. My grandparents remained with me even now, in my memory, in my heart, and in the many ways they'd inspired me during our time together.

TWENTY-THREE

Like the winter, spring came early. Surely Hua Chi would arrive soon—if she was coming at all. I started to feel restless again, aware once more that this school, this farm, was a way station, not my ultimate destination.

One night I stayed up to complete the writing. I wasn't prepared for it to end so soon, but I was able to transcribe the final section almost word for word. In an apparent window of lucidity and burst of energy, Socrates must also have poured out his final words in frenzied moments of inspiration, completing his work before relinquishing it to the mountain.

Both conventional and transcendental states of awareness have value. If you can't find peace here in daily life, you won't find it elsewhere. Reaching beyond the conventional mind-set isn't an act of will but of remembrance. When you've experienced deep relaxation, it's easier to return to that state. The same holds true once you've tasted the transcendent.

Even in moments of elevated awareness, you'll need to take out the trash and do the laundry. So even in the midst of everyday life—as you do what you do according to all that has shaped you—you'd be wise to live as if time exists, so you can keep an organized calendar. Live as if you make conscious choices, so you can take responsibility for them. Live as if accidents happen, so you can stay vigilant. Live as if you're an independent individual, so you fully appreciate your innate worth and singular destiny. And live as if death is real, so that you can savor the precious opportunity that is life on planet Earth.

Until you experience transcendent truths directly, stay open to the possibility. You can bridge conventional and transcendental awareness whenever you remember to shift awareness from one to the other, according to the needs of the moment. In the meantime, keep faith with paradox, humor, and change, and honor the illusions that still apply in everyday life.

It has never been easy to rise above circumstance and appreciate the perfection of life unfolding. Much of the time your attention will, quite appropriately, remain focused on everyday duties. But now and then, remember your sense of balance, perspective, and humor—they are the better parts of wisdom.

Welcome to the realm of flesh and spirit, and to the truths that animate each of them. Welcome home.

With these final words, my work was complete, my part in all this finished, at least for the present. And when I reread all I had written—surprised to see only twenty pages of handwritten text—I experienced those words not as their author but rather as the translator of my mentor's insights.

As I sat at that small desk on a farm in a forest across the world from my home, I had to face the fact that my own awareness, perhaps like most people's, was focused mostly on the conventional level. But also like most people, I had a yearning to transcend, a longing for some kind of liberation. Which, I supposed, lay at the core of all religious and spiritual paths. Other than the occasional glimpses and visions generated by Socrates in years past, or through meditation or psychedelics or other mystical means, I had no direct access to the transcendent states to which he referred, except through that shift of attention, that act of remembering.

I knew that serious philosophers, physicists, and psychologists have written in exquisite and sometimes excruciating detail about the nature of time, choice, the self, and death from various viewpoints. But Soc's understanding of paradox—the nature of conventional and transcendental truths—was the first model I had found to reconcile these contradictory views about reality. I could only hope that these existential insights, as I had articulated them, might inform the lives of others as they had informed my own. I was still a work in progress, but now I'd glimpsed new possibilities.

Two days later, as the sun disappeared over the mountains, I stepped into the stream and sat under the waterfall Chun Han and I had built, letting the waters pound on my head and shoulders, cleansing body and mind. Through the cur-

tain of water descending around me, I heard laughter and Chun Han's hoarse bark.

Later that evening we gathered to celebrate the coming of spring. Everywhere I looked I saw colored lights, sizzling fireworks, dazzling costumes, and whirling acrobats—my students. I wasn't the coach tonight. Under Chun Han's direction, they sprang into the air again and again, celebrating their freedom from the usual bonds of gravity.

A group of my students took me by the arms and led me in a wild dance. Their faces shining, the young men and women twirled round and round, singing a Chinese chant over and over until I lost myself in the lights and laughter, floating off the floor of the pavilion where everyone now seemed lighter than air. And somewhere in the distance I heard a few of them singing, "Row, row, row your boat, gently down the stream. . . ."

As I walked back toward my quiet loft in the early-morning hours, I could still hear the sounds of the mandolin, the flute, the dutar, and the drum, rising up into the night sky, floating up toward a moon as bright and yellow as yak's cheese. On impulse, I wandered over to the water feature I now thought of as Chun Han Fall, to get one last look at the leaping waters in the light of the lanterns and a setting moon.

I had my own reason to celebrate, having completed

the writing mission that had formed the backdrop of my time here, accomplishing something that had seemed impossible a few months before when I'd first found Soc's letter. I felt as if the great river of the Tao had carried me like a leaf down its shifting currents.

Sometimes those currents take a sharp turn.

The following day, after the evening meal, I returned to my loft and reached into the knapsack for the journals as I'd done so many times, looking forward to reading through them again.

Perplexed, I emptied the pack. Then I searched every inch of the loft. Twice. It made no sense, but I had to acknowledge that it had happened: both Soc's journal and my own had vanished without a trace.

TWENTY-FOUR

I wish I could say that the months of training and writing had left me with an abiding sense of nonattachment and prepared me to accept this loss with grace. But at that moment such a state of detachment felt idealistic and beyond my capacity. As self-critical thoughts assailed me—*Why didn't I photocopy Soc's journal in Hong Kong when I had the chance? Why didn't I think of hand-copying each page as I wrote?*—emotions and adrenaline flooded my body.

I must have misplaced the journals, I thought. This notion triggered another round of furious (and fruitless) searching. *I could have walked in my sleep and left them somewhere.* No, I'd seen the journals earlier that morning. I now understood how Socrates must have felt when he recovered from his fever without the journal or any clear sense of its location.

Who could have taken them? I wondered. It made no sense. No one at the farm had any reason to take them, or any knowledge of the journals in the first place. No one, except for Mei Bao, could even read them, and she had only to ask. I pictured her face and the faces of Chun Han, Master Ch'an, and my students. As I meditated on each of their faces, my body calmed. The panic and anger, having reached a pitch of intensity, subsided. And as my body relaxed, so did my mind. Finally I accepted reality: The journals weren't here. I had no idea where they were. Nothing would happen during the night. With that, I gave myself to sleep.

On my way to find Mei Bao early the next morning, I stopped short as a familiar figure with white-streaked hair and clad in a tracksuit mounted the steps of the main house. "Hua Chi!" I called out and rushed forward.

She turned and smiled, saying, "Such an enthusiastic American-style greeting!" Hearing that, I stopped and bowed. She took a long, approving look at me. "You look well, Dan. I would have come sooner but for the frost. We'll depart in a few days."

"Hua Chi, I have to tell—"

"We'll speak soon, Dan. No doubt you have much to share. But first I must pay respects to my brother and to Mei Bao."

Not to be deterred from her purpose, Hua Chi turned

and disappeared through the beaded curtain, where those who might have answers to my dilemma were now sequestered. I reluctantly left to join the morning work duty. I wasn't even sure what I would tell her first, given everything that had occurred during her long absence. I decided I would start with the disappearance of my journals.

I'd been trying to convince myself that the loss of Soc's journal and my notebook didn't ultimately matter. The world didn't go spinning off its axis—only my world, my goals. The event itself, the missing journals, was fact. It was my reaction to the loss that preoccupied me.

A short time later, Hua Chi found me and invited me to stroll with her around the farm's perimeter. As we skirted the edge of the forest, she began, "My brother and Mei Bao are pleased with you both as a student and as a teacher. Whatever may happen in the future, you've made a contribution."

I spoke more rapidly than I'd intended: "I'm glad to hear that, Hua Chi, and so glad to see you, but back in Hong Kong I told you about a journal I'd found. I've been writing a longer version, considerable work, and a day or two ago the original journal and my own notebook went missing. I can't understand—"

"Oh, don't trouble yourself about that," she said with a casual wave of her hand. "They're perfectly safe. In good hands. I just borrowed them."

I froze in place at the far end of a newly planted field. Hua Chi stopped as well, as if to admire the work of the farmers. Suffering from tunnel vision, I was in no state to admire or even see anything around us. Hearing her words, I felt relieved, furious, mystified, speechless. But not for long. "You *what*?" I said. "But why? When were you going to tell me?"

"Oh, I thought it best to see what happened first."

What kind of riddle was this? Had Papa Joe shape-shifted into her likeness? At that moment, it wouldn't have surprised me. Nothing would. I could barely get two words out: "Explain. Please."

Hua Chi shrugged pleasantly, relaxed as usual, and, resuming her walk back toward the dining hall, said, "Those months ago, over tea, Dan, you mentioned a journal—and that someone was looking for it."

"Yes, I remember."

"And do you also recall giving me a piece of paper with a woman's name, and a telephone number?"

"Yes, but what does that have to do with—"

"I called the number a few nights later and reached the woman, Ama. Her voice expressed strength and kindness. I gave her your message about finding the journal. She sounded sincerely pleased, even excited for you. So I introduced myself and told her the circumstances of our first meeting, and how I had made your travel arrangements. She thanked me, and we said good-bye."

"Thank you for doing that. But I still don't see—"

"About ten days later, during my morning practice in the park, I noticed a man watching our group from a respectful distance. He had trained in the martial arts; that much I could tell from the way he stood. When we finished the form, he asked if anyone in our group knew a woman named Hua Chi. I told him that I was reasonably familiar with such a woman, and asked him what interest he had in her—one can't be too careful."

She continued as we walked behind the pavilion, entered the dining hall, and sat in the far corner near the exit to continue this private conversation. "As it turned out, he was the man you cautioned me about—rightly, I think. He told me he was determined to find the man who had the journal, to do whatever it took to find and retrieve it. He seemed certain that 'this Hua Chi woman' was a link to fulfilling his mission. So, continuing my little intrigue, I told him that I could arrange a meeting the next morning. Early. In the park, before practice."

We each filled a plate and a bowl with vegetables and porridge, the usual meal. Then we returned to our seats. Hua Chi set down her plate and bowl and continued her story. "He seemed only mildly surprised to see me there, alone. I think he'd suspected me all along. We talked. I made a decision that may yet find a good resolution."

"Would that resolution have anything to do with returning my journals?" I asked.

"I think so," she answered. "But that's not for me to say. You see, he asked to speak with you directly."

"Ah, well," I said, not without sarcasm, "you can just give me his phone number when we return to Hong Kong."

"Oh, that won't be necessary," she said, pointing behind me, over my shoulder. "He accompanied me here."

I turned to see the man I knew as Pájaro framed by the exit door. In his hands he held the journals.

Hua Chi rose, her plate untouched, and left us alone.

TWENTY-FIVE

He wore an old pair of jeans, a T-shirt, and a cap with a red star, like my own. When our eyes met, he looked down. He stood as if waiting for permission to come forward. When he finally approached, he held out the journal and my notebook, setting them on the table in front of me. He sat across from me, in the place vacated by Hua Chi. His gaze still downward, he said, "I'm sorry for the trouble I've caused you, Dan."

"You've read the journals," I said, on high alert, considering our last encounter.

He nodded, and then spoke softly. "First I read the notes written by your teacher. They made sense only after I read your . . . translation." He paused then, as if searching back in time. "If I'd taken the real journal from you on the mountain, I wouldn't have understood anything." Then: "I regret striking you. At the time, I didn't see any other way. . . ."

As my questions jockeyed for position at the front of the line, Pájaro looked up, and we made real eye contact for the first time. "I don't know how to thank you—or how to compensate you for what I did."

I said the first thing that came to mind: "Well, you did leave me the five dollars."

We both smiled. And that's how I came to share a meal with the man who had pursued me across the world, and who I had believed intended me great bodily harm if we ever met again. As my students looked on from a distance, shy but ever curious, Pájaro began to explain what had driven him.

"Thirty years ago, my father was driving to work when he saw a man stumbling along the roadway—"

I interjected. "Pájaro, I know that your father gave Socrates a ride and took him to an infirmary. I also know about your dad's illness and passing. . . ."

Bewildered, he asked, "How did you—?"

"Soon after I arrived in Albuquerque," I said, "I found a schoolteacher named Ama. Her father, the doctor who treated Socrates, had told her a story many years before, about the gardener who sought his counsel and who was seeking a journal. I helped her recall that story. So I can understand your father's desperate search. But why you, after all these years? And how did you know about me?"

"After my father's death," he said, "I raised myself with the help of an aunt who let me stay in her back room and raid her fridge in return for yard work. I grew up pretty wild—studied survival skills, learned to track and hunt. I cleaned the bathrooms and mats at a local karate school in exchange for classes. I did well in sports but spent most of my time alone, preparing myself."

"For what?"

"My father's mission—it gave me a purpose, I suppose. I vowed not to die like him. I came to believe that if I found the journal, I might not die at all. . . ."

He shook his head. "I don't know what I was thinking. Striving for physical immortality would make perfect sense if people stopped having children. But as things stand, if such a secret were discovered, only the wealthy would have access to it, or it would create a chaotic, overpopulated world."

He's right, I thought. *At some point the elderly need to die and be recycled—it's the house rules, as Soc would say. Love of life is one thing. Fear of death is quite another.*

"But that doesn't explain how you found me and followed me—or how you found Hua Chi."

"Ama, the woman you met. She told me all about you—everything I needed to know."

A shiver passed through me. A bitter, metallic taste of betrayal constricted my throat. I had to ask: "Did you have to force her, or was she glad to tell you everything?"

He smiled and waved away my concern. "Nothing like that, Dan. I've known Ama for years. She doesn't know I was the gardener's son. To her, I'm just a friend and confidant."

My eyes widened. "Oh my God—*you're Joe Stalking Wolf?*" I sat there in shock. Why hadn't I realized it! Ama wouldn't have guessed because she hadn't even recalled the story about the gardener's son until she told me.

Joe Stalking Wolf, aka Pájaro, continued: "Fifteen years after my father's death, I joined the local police. I used a legal excuse to access the infirmary records and found the name of the doctor who'd treated the mysterious stranger years before. Ama's father. He had died, but I found his daughter. . . .

"It took me a year to gain her confidence," he said. "She had no idea I was seeking the journal. To her I was just a good listener. After you visited the school, she called me. It was just a news item, the kind of thing we shared with each other."

I thought back to something I'd heard, that there are only two kinds of stories: *Either a stranger comes to town or someone goes on a quest. My story qualifies on both counts*, I realized. Ama had told her friend about me, the stranger. And this story was getting stranger all the time. . . .

Still trying to take this in, I couldn't stop myself from asking: "Your relationship with Ama—was it only about the journal?"

"At first. But over time—" The next moment, when he grasped my reason for asking, his face broke into a smile. "Ama and I are good friends, Dan, but not in the way you might think. As it happens, Ama prefers the intimate company of other women."

I felt like slapping my forehead. *So much for my powers of observation.*

Joe Stalking Wolf went on to explain how, using high-power binoculars, he'd observed me at the service station. *What is it with me and service stations?* I thought. He drove ahead of me, left his vehicle, and waited by the road as the hitchhiker, businessman, and travel guide Pájaro. He'd intended to stick with me until I found the journal, but when he saw Papa Joe inside the café, he knew it was too risky. "He's Ama's oldest friend, and he'd met me before. He could have recognized my voice—or my scent."

"Blind as a bat, smart as a fox," I said, mostly to myself.

Joe Stalking Wolf smiled again. "You got that right."

Then, more serious, he slumped over like a lost boy. "I'm not a bad person, Dan. Taking that journal was an act of desperation, a life's ambition. I've lived my father's dream for so long that I have none of my own. I have no idea what to do now."

Feeling like a washrag that had been wrung out to dry, I wondered what I could say to help this man. "Well," I managed, presuming that we'd both be heading back to Hong Kong with Hua Chi, "you could stay here for a few days. Maybe help in the fields."

Shaking his head, he said, "No, I can't accept their hospitality. Not yet. I haven't earned it. I'll stay in the forest for a few days. I have some thinking to do—about what you wrote. And about my life, eternal or not. Your words opened my eyes and mind wider with each reading. I wish my father could have seen it."

He would have died just the same, I thought, *as we all do, no matter what our beliefs or philosophies. All of us, heading for Samarra. . . .*

Before I could say anything else to Joe Stalking Wolf, he rose and excused himself. I suddenly noticed that, despite what must have been profound hunger, he hadn't touched his food.

TWENTY-SIX

With the journals back in my loft, I continued pondering the turn of events until Hua Chi joined me as I headed to the pavilion to teach one of my last acrobatics sessions. "You've received high praise from my brother," she said, "not only for your diligent practice, but for instructing and inspiring your students."

Glad to hear this, since Master Ch'an had given no outward sign of approval, I said, "It's been a great opportunity. I just wish . . ."

"What?"

"I had hoped to work with him more directly, but I understand how the language barrier made that difficult—"

"Without Mei Bao," she added.

"Of course. What would your brother do without her support?"

Hua Chi chuckled. "True enough, but not in the way you may think."

"What?"

"My brother is indeed a master—a master gardener and farmer. He studied martial arts in his twenties but realized that it wasn't his true calling. The bones of this place, and the blood, are his. But the spirit, well—has Mei Bao told you the story of how we met?"

"Yes."

"But she's too modest. Did she tell you how quickly she mastered the t'ai chi forms, or how greatly she surpassed my modest skills before she'd even reached her eighteenth year?"

"Really? I had no idea."

"My brother and I conceived the idea of inviting worthy orphans to help develop a self-sufficient farm. Only after Mei Bao's arrival here did she discover in herself a desire to share her gifts with others. To teach. Out of her desire, the school began. After her arrival, even the forest changed."

At the entrance to the pavilion, Hua Chi said, "My brother is as devoted to Mei Bao as she is to him. I'm not surprised that she acknowledged him as the source of her wisdom. But make no mistake about it, Mei Bao is the Master of Taishan Forest."

It had been a day of revelations, from which I was still reeling.

As we entered the pavilion, Hua Chi added, "Your teacher, Socrates, he told you to find a hidden school."

"Yes, but he didn't say where. So I was headed to Japan. . . ."

"I was wondering: Did he tell you to *study* at a hidden school?"

"What else could he have meant?"

Hua Chi only smiled, letting my question float away as she joined Mei Bao and Master Ch'an, both of whom had appeared to observe what would be my last acrobatics class in the Taishan Forest.

During our session, I caught a glimpse of Joe Stalking Wolf watching from the forest cover. I expected that Hua Chi noticed as well. That evening I found myself thinking again about him. *My first reader.* Before I showed the journal to anyone else, I decided to read it one more time.

Late that night, as I read the final sentences by lamplight, a weight lifted from my shoulders. I sensed that Socrates would approve. I hoped to tell him about it someday soon, and show him what I'd written. He couldn't know it then, nor did I, but this collaboration between us marked the beginning of my writing life.

In the process, I'd learned that reading was one way to absorb ideas, writing quite another. My creative struggle to clarify Soc's journal notes called forth a deeper understanding. But I had merely understood. As Soc once told me, "Realization comes only from direct experience." I had to face the reality that the insights I'd expressed had not yet penetrated me. They were still slogans, words on a page, thoughts in my head, notions and ideas. But they were also seeds that would blossom in their own time. For now, I could only accept my current reality and wait for a ripening.

With that acceptance, I finally settled down to sleep in the early-morning hours. As I lay there, I thought about how sometimes life more closely resembled improvisational comedy than strategic planning. I had no idea what the future might hold. Like Papa Joe, and that line in Corinthians, I'd lived "by faith, not by sight."

TWENTY-SEVEN

While working the field the next morning, I saw two strangers emerge from the forest—older men, dressed in gray high-collar tunics, soiled and frayed. With serious faces, they scanned the fields and buildings. Two other men joined them, wearing military garb and carrying Kalashnikov carbines. The bell that usually signaled the midday meal sounded behind me, again and again.

I turned to see Mei Bao approaching with Master Ch'an, followed by Chun Han and the remaining students. I'd been digging a trench and was still holding the shovel.

The two soldiers held their rifles at the ready. One of the two older men spoke loudly—as if he had authority over all of us. Mei Bao, who now stood just behind me, whispered a translation in my ear: "The People's Proletariat

Central Committee of Heilongjiang has learned of this unauthorized farm and school for . . ."—Mei Bao paused in her translation—"for spies." It was the first time I'd ever seen her lose her composure.

The older man scanned our small group until his eyes fixed on me. He spoke again, with Mei Bao translating in my ear. "I see proof," he said, pointing to me. "An imperialist running dog"—*there it was!*—"here to train you as agents of a foreign government. I require his entry papers, but I don't expect to find them."

That's when Hua Chi stepped forward to speak, and Mei Bao continued to translate: "This visitor is a teacher of acrobatics, nothing more," she said. "If you'll just let me get them, I have his papers, authorizing a temporary visit to help these orphaned children learn a skill so they may contribute to the people's culture. Whoever told you there are any agents here is misinformed or deceiving the people's government."

"That's a serious accusation," said the man, speaking more quietly now, as Hua Chi neared him. "Nonetheless," he went on, "rather than seeking the right attitude and contributing to the common good, all persons here have separated themselves from their countrymen, selfishly hoarding goods, making no contribution of crops to the larger community. Where are your permits to farm or to teach?" he shouted. "You might have been able to secretly continue this degraded life if you hadn't been so foolish as to bring a foreign intruder here."

Mei Bao sounded reluctant to translate this last part. *It's my fault*, I thought, horrified. *Someone must have seen me when I went with Mei Bao to the village.*

At that point a fifth stranger stepped out of the forest, younger than the rest. He wore similar Mao-inspired garb. He looked angry, but I sensed something else: Fear? Shame?

"Chang Li," whispered Mei Bao. *The student who ran away*, I recalled. She shook her head sadly. "He must have led them here."

The older spokesman gestured to Chang Li, then placed his hands on the boy's shoulders. "So you see, through the heroism and patriotism of this young proletariat leader, we know what you're up to. You can't hide any longer!" He gestured to the two armed military men, who stepped forward. "I'm here to take over temporary leadership of this communal farm, which will now become a re-education camp. More laborers will soon arrive. The young workers will stay on. The farmwork will continue as before, but this 'school,' as you call it, has no place in the People's Republic."

I sensed that Mei Bao was finding it difficult to repeat his words, but she continued until the spokesman pointed to Master Ch'an, Hua Chi, Mei Bao, and me.

"The four of you," he said, "will come with us back to Taishan Village and then to Beijing, where you will be interrogated and judged. If found guilty, you'll be taken to a detention house. If your error is deemed a political misjudgment, once you're reeducated you'll be allowed to rejoin society. But the foreigner, papers or not, he will be—"

Out of the corner of my eye, I saw Master Ch'an fall to his knees. I stared, unbelieving, as he crawled forward. Mei Bao rushed forward to help the defeated old man stand slowly before the leader. Hua Chi, looking suddenly old herself, leaned on Chun Han, and limped forward toward the men. The armed soldiers looked confused; they half-raised their rifles—

Too late. Mei Bao moved with lightning speed. She must have pushed the chest of one soldier; I saw him go flying backward. He slammed into a nearby tree trunk and fell to the ground. Chun Han ran toward the fallen man. At nearly the same instant, Master Ch'an and Hua Chi had somehow disabled the other soldier, knocking him out as well.

A third soldier stepped out of the forest, raised his Kalashnikov and took aim at Hua Chi and her brother. Then two things happened at once: Chun Han leapt forward to shield Ch'an and Hua Chi. And Joe Stalking Wolf appeared out of nowhere, slamming one foot into the soldier's spine and sending him sprawling as the shot went awry. Joe pinned the soldier to the ground with one knee and slammed a handheld stone into the back of his head, knocking him unconscious. For a moment it looked like he was going to hit the man again, then he glanced over. Our eyes met. He dropped the stone.

TWENTY-EIGHT

The authorities, the soldiers, and Chang Li, who had betrayed us all, now looked out on drastically different circumstances. The two older men both began to talk at once, sputtering. As the students' attention shifted toward them, my eyes moved across the farm. I recognized the moment for what it was: the beginning of the end.

I saw Chun Han on his knees with both hands pressed against his ribs. As I approached, he pulled his hands away from his body as if to greet me. They were covered in blood. The wild shot had penetrated his upper abdomen just below the heart. He quickly slipped into unconsciousness and was still.

Mei Bao reached him the same time I did. Her face twisted with grief as she cradled his body.

"Chun Han!" we called. But he couldn't respond. Not ever.

One by one, the students became aware of what had happened. One after another, they began to weep, as a collective sorrow took hold. Out of the corner of my eye, I saw Joe Stalking Wolf hand a rifle to Hua Chi, and together they moved toward the authorities.

I knew I should do something, but I couldn't move. Only a few minutes before, working peacefully in the field, I'd waved to Chun Han as he passed. Gentle Chun Han, my friend from the beginning.

I became vaguely aware, lost as I was in reminiscences and regrets, that Master Ch'an was moving among the students, squeezing shoulders, speaking quiet words. Following Master Ch'an's lead, the students surrounded the authorities and a miserable Chang Li, and dragged the unconscious soldiers into the circle. The representatives of the People's Republic of China were now surrounded by the students.

Mei Bao directed a few other students as they lifted Chun Han's large body and carried it back toward the main house, with everyone else following behind. I glanced toward Joe Stalking Wolf, his eyes still on the forest, a gun in his hand, following our small group and the larger cadre of students prodding the authorities toward the pavilion.

I learned later that the intruders were locked in a storage shed. Hua Chi told me that the spokesman had promised "serious consequences" if they were not allowed to return and report to their committee. Joe now insisted on sitting vigil outside until Master Ch'an and the others decided what to do.

I sat down next to him. He'd found a purpose suited to his experience. I suddenly felt like the outsider. Somehow I knew that before I left the school, the school would leave me.

TWENTY-NINE

That evening, Mei Bao and Hua Chi washed and wrapped Chun Han's body. The advanced students came together as pallbearers and bore the remains to a site on the far side of the crystal pond, under an emerald canopy of leaves. After a short ceremony, we buried our friend. His resting place was unmarked, hidden as the school had been, to remain undisturbed.

Much later, after the students had retired, Hua Chi invited me to join Master Ch'an and Mei Bao in the main house. As they shared stories of Chun Han, I half-expected to turn and see him by my side.

I heard someone call my name. Mei Bao was speaking to me, though she seemed far away: ". . . with or without your presence here, these men would have come."

Hua Chi added, "Mei Bao and my brother have

planned for such a possibility. Even the timing wasn't entirely unexpected, since Mei Bao had noticed someone watching her last time she went to Taishan Village."

"They must have seen me," I said dully.

Hua Chi put her hand on my shoulder. "This isn't about you, Dan! A few months before your arrival, Chang Li became romantically obsessed with Mei Bao. She rebuffed him. He ran away soon after. The rest you know."

Thinking about Chun Han, and about what this might mean for all of them, I felt tears stinging my eyes. "What will happen?" I asked.

Hua Chi offered one view. "It seems to me that our lives unfold in a mysterious way. Since meaning is a human invention, let's make a positive meaning of this experience!"

The following day, she opened the shed and released the captives. She even gave them a little dried fruit, some small cakes, and enough water for their journey. Master Ch'an and Mei Bao chose to remain in seclusion until the intruders departed.

Just before they disappeared into the forest, I heard the spokesman shout something at Hua Chi. I didn't need her to translate. Since they had found their way here with Chang Li's help, it was likely they would find their way back and make good on whatever threat he'd shouted.

"You and I will be gone long before then," Hua Chi said.

"But what about everyone else?" I asked. "What about the school?" My arm swept toward the dormitory, the fields, the pavilion.

"They'll rebuild the school in another remote location," she said. "Even in a populous country like China, there are places of sanctuary, if you know how to find them. Joe Stalking Wolf just told me that he'll go with them."

As we walked back toward the main house, Hua Chi stopped, turned to me, and said emphatically, as a form of tough love, I suppose: "You have been a welcome guest, Dan—a visitor, a fellow worker, and a teacher. I know you made friends and won't forget your students. But this wasn't your home. They don't need your help or service any longer."

Time sped up after that. It wasn't easy to say good-bye to Mei Bao or to Master Ch'an—and all the more difficult to say good-bye to my students. But our farewells were brief since they were all fully occupied with arrangements to which I was not privy. I also said good-bye to Joe Stalking Wolf, and promised him I'd tell Ama the whole story, as best I could, and convey his fond regards.

My sleep was filled with a tumult of movement. When I awoke and stepped outside, the farm was empty. They had all vanished like a mirage.

Hua Chi found me sitting in the empty pavilion. "So you see," she said, "they really were prepared to leave on short notice. We are the last to go."

What a shame, I thought. *Gross injustice—petty bureaucrats and so-called revolutionary ideology!* I didn't know whether to feel sad or furious—probably a mixture of both. They had devoted so much to this place.

I recalled the story Socrates had told me about the monk Hakuin, who was wrongly accused of fathering a child with a young girl. When villagers insisted he raise the child, he said only three words as he took the child in his arms: "Is that so?" Two years later, the girl and the young father asked for the child back. His response was the same. He received and let go without resistance. This transcendent capacity still eluded me as I surveyed the empty fields and silent pavilion that had nourished so much life and learning.

Hua Chi and I bypassed Taishan Village for a larger town to catch a small steam train. At the station, I asked, "Do you really have official papers for me?"

In a silent reply, she handed me an envelope with documents. Then she said, "You've given much to my brother's community. A part of you will remain with them. That much, at least, I foresaw."

And they will remain with me, I thought. Speaking it aloud would have sounded trivial, so I remained silent.

Hua Chi cautioned me to keep a low profile on the trip

back to Hong Kong. Even in the warming spring, I was covered in traditional clothing and a traditional conical hat, pulled down low over my eyes so my face was in shadow.

The butter-colored air of spring thickened as we traveled south, rolling past small villages, past the Celestial Mountains to the east. "The mountains are home to the snow leopard and to wolves that migrate down from Mongolia," Hua Chi whispered, still the consummate travel guide. I too now viewed such creatures as Guardians. And I wondered what would become of Hong Hong, the forest bear.

My thoughts were interrupted by Hua Chi, who spoke softly, her English accent muffled by the sounds of the train: "I'm fascinated by nature, but I couldn't live out in the country."

No television reception, I thought, discovering that I could still smile.

Far behind us lay the mystical Pamir region, where Socrates had studied with Nada (then María) and the others—a place threaded by the ancient Silk Road, where Hindu, Islamic, and Chinese cultures traded goods and stories. To the southwest lay the towering peaks of Tibet and Nepal. I peered at a curve of track ahead and saw, through a haze of yellow clay, straw grids to fend off the ever-encroaching dunes of dust.

The next day we entered the Shanxi region, called the Middle Kingdom in ancient times, the wellspring of Chinese civilization. As we steamed past the broad Yellow River and the Fen, Hua Chi said, "These great rivers were known as China's sorrow as well as China's pride. They gave life along the shores, but when they flooded, thousands died and many more lost crops and homes. China's history, like many, I suppose, is a bittersweet one."

That evening we caught a ferry from Guangzhou to Hong Kong. That was the only point when an official gave us any trouble. He held us back, eyeing me suspiciously. But after President Nixon's visit to China just a few years before, and the country's new contact with a larger world, foreigners were treated with more courtesy. So, with a severe nod, the official finally let me pass. Only then did Hua Chi follow. I felt the relief shared by most travelers returning to a more familiar culture and language. I spent that night at Hua Chi's home.

When I woke the next morning, the first thing I saw was David Carradine's face—she'd hung the poster to celebrate our mutual enthusiasm. After tea and some breakfast, I joined her in the park for a little push hands. She seemed pleased at my modest improvement. We exchanged bows. I looked into her eyes for the last time before shouldering my knapsack and heading for the airport.

A few hours later, through the aircraft window, I surveyed the coast of Hong Kong and the vast land of China across the harbor and beyond. Only then did it strike me that I'd never given Hua Chi the journal to read. And she'd never asked. *How important are these words on paper, given all that has happened?* I thought. *Will the words ever matter?* I'd never know unless I shared them someday.

Now Japan lay before me. Socrates had once told me to follow my nose and trust my instincts. So that's what I would do.

PART THREE

Stones, Roots, Water

Die in your mind every morning
and you will no longer fear death.

YAMAMOTO TSUNETOMO,
HAGAKURE: BOOK OF THE SAMURAI

THIRTY

After arriving in Osaka, I was now en route to Kyoto, two hours away by train. Japan's ancient capital, Kyoto reflected Shinto and Buddhist traditions still resonant in the city's abundant temples, gardens, teahouses, and castles, where samurai once guarded and served the emperor.

In the customs line I overheard someone say, "Kyoto has a thousand temples and ten thousand bars." *So much for ancient traditions,* I thought.

From the train station I called a small hotel in central Kyoto and booked a room. Noting the name and address, I caught a taxi. It looked new and unusually clean. The white-gloved driver took pride in his work and made a good first impression. Using what little Japanese I knew, I directed him toward the hotel: *"Hoteru Sunomo no hana, kudasai."*

"Hai—arigato," replied the driver. He seemed pleased at my modest attempt to speak his language. We took off like a shot. I noticed he was young, and like many young drivers he worked the edges of the speed limit. I almost told him to slow down, but didn't know how to say it. I wish I had tried.

We were just entering the city center. I scanned the sights ahead. As we approached an intersection, I saw a motorcycle rider with a passenger dart out from a side street. The driver was glancing the other way. "Watch out!" I yelled, less than two seconds before the right fender of the taxi smashed at full speed into the motorcycle. The sound was horrific and the sight worse. The bike spun wildly, and both riders were thrown into the air as the taxi came screeching to a halt. Reflexively, both the taxi driver and I jumped out and ran to the two fallen riders. My legs felt rubbery—not only from what had just occurred, but because of the memory flash of my own motorcycle crash nine years earlier. I felt sick.

Then time sped up as we drew near a young woman, bloodied, crying, and rocking back and forth from the pain of likely broken bones and other injuries. She wore a helmet, which a bystander carefully removed. It was most likely the driver's helmet, since he had none. He lay absolutely still, his body a distorted tangle. One look at his bloody, smashed-in head told us he was probably dead.

The clerk of a nearby store had run back inside to call for help. Soon we heard sirens.

I stayed at the scene long enough to tell the police that we had had the green light and that the motorcycle had shot out from the side street directly into our path. The young taxi driver looked ashen and bowed to me again and again in apology. I gave the officer the name of my hotel in case they needed to ask me anything else, then found another taxi. I hardly remember anything more until I arrived at my hotel.

Shaken, I checked in, entered my room, unrolled the traditional futon bed on the tatami-mat floor, and lay down. It was the second death I'd witnessed in the space of one week.

This fatal collision seemed like a dark omen, as if the reaper were right next to me, whispering words I couldn't grasp. I lay there, my mind whirling. I tried to make plans, but then thought, *Why make plans when plans change? What plans had that young taxi driver made, or the couple on the motorcycle? And why have I come here, anyway? Have I misread the message of the little samurai?*

At some point in the night, the black-hooded specter who'd haunted me during my college days in Berkeley returned to point a bony finger. It could take me. Anytime. Anywhere. I knew that now.

The next morning, I awoke in a better mental state but

somber—echoes and images of yesterday's events still with me. No longer second-guessing whether I should have come to Japan, I accepted my reality: I *was* here, so I would visit a few martial arts schools and make some notes for my report to the grant committee. Then I would head home.

After checking directions with the bellman, who spoke some English, I ate a Japanese-style breakfast: miso soup, rice, pickles, and dumplings. Then I set out to explore the city and attend to professional business.

As a youth, and later during my years coaching at Stanford, I'd studied enough karate and aikido to know which questions to ask. My recent t'ai chi training also gave me more sensitive eyes for perceiving the flows of energy underlying the physical techniques.

I visited a well-known karate school first. After observing a class, I was able to speak with the head instructor through one of his students. This aging *sensei* fit the picture of a karate veteran, with his graying hair, chiseled cheekbones, and flattened knuckles. He wore a sturdy cotton uniform—a traditional *gi*—tied with a faded and worn black belt. *The older the belt, the greater the experience*, I reminded myself.

I'd observed the instructor demonstrating and sparring with another black belt during the class. He'd seemed a formidable fighter, but he spoke in a gentle voice. As the student translated, the *sensei* related one version of karate history. His voice faded in and out as my focus wavered; I was still shaken and preoccupied with the deaths of my friend Chun Han back in China and of the motorcyclist the day before. Does every death remind us of our own?

Meanwhile, the *sensei* spoke of a journey undertaken by the Indian prince Bodhidharma, who traveled from India to China spreading Buddhism and martial training, especially among the Shaolin monks. He devised a system of martial movements to promote vitality after hours of meditation and to serve as self-defense from bullies or bandits, a style which came to be known as Shaolin temple boxing. According to the legend, in doing so, he knit together karate, Asian martial arts, and Buddhist meditation.

Having observed and made notes for my report, I bowed and took my leave.

Later that afternoon, I made my way to a satellite school of the aikido headquarters. Finding no one in the entryway or small office, I removed my shoes and stepped quietly into the tatami-floored practice hall, or *dojo*, which means place or school of the way. There I came upon a somber scene: The students knelt in rows facing the traditional altar and image of Morihei Ueshiba, the founder of aikido. At the head of the room knelt four senior instructors in the traditional *seiza* posture. They were dressed in the white cotton tops and black skirtlike *hakama* pants of elder instructors. Their students also knelt in stunned silence as one of the instructors carefully folded up a piece of parchment from which he had been reading. I noticed several students crying softly. *Sad news. Perhaps a death,* I thought. *Another death.*

My mind and heart flashed back to the pond in Taishan Forest as Chun Han's body went into the earth. I sat on a low bench in the back of the room and listened to yet another language I couldn't understand. *Stop feeling sorry for yourself,* said a voice in my head. *You don't speak Japanese, Dan, but you speak the language of martial arts.*

True enough, and I did recognize the instructor's next words to his students: "*Renshu shite kudasai—onegaishimasu!*" His tone was warm but emphatic. *Please continue practicing—carry on!* I thought, translating to myself.

The students rose quickly, wiping at their eyes as they formed into pairs, doing their best to show *gaman*, or stoic forbearance, a facet of the Japanese character I'd come to understand during my aikido training. They took turns circling one another, staying alert and relaxed, moving in for random attacks, which enabled their partners to practice a variety of flowing, circular defenses, mostly involving wrist locks and leveraged throws, turning the momentum of the attack seamlessly into a controlled defense that neutralized the attack without seriously injuring the attacker.

One of the instructors approached me, and I thought I

heard him say something in English. I turned to him and asked, "Please, *kudasai*, what has happened?"

At first he said nothing—he might have been searching for the right words or deciding whether to share the news with a foreign visitor. In slow, fractured English, he explained that their esteemed chief instructor, a seventh-degree black belt and the founder of that *dojo*, had recently taken his own life.

A chill wind blew through me. For an instant, the *sensei* before me was replaced by the hooded specter. *Everywhere I go, death stalks me,* I thought. And I wondered, *Am I the servant forever fleeing to Samarra?* In answer, a phrase from Socrates came to mind: "There is no victory over death, only the realization of who we really are." *What does that mean?* I shouted internally.

Before he took his leave, seeing the expression on my face, the *sensei* added, "He did not practice *seppuku* in the manner of the samurai. There was no dishonor. Sensei Nakayama, a teacher of great strength and wisdom, had deep sadness. A depression. I read a message he wrote to the students—to encourage them to practice sincerely, before he departed for Aokigahara Jukai."

"Aokigahara Jukai—what's that?" I asked, but the instructor didn't appear to hear me. He bowed and departed. So I returned to my seat to observe. Even in their grief, the students guided one another with attacks and defenses in a graceful dance of power, where harmony was lost and restored again and again.

With everything that had happened—including learning that a master of aikido had just taken his own life—I left in a daze. *Energy fields,* I thought as I pushed open the door and stepped out into the hazy sunlight and humid air of spring. I wandered the streets after that, seeing little, recalling nothing.

In the early evening, back in my hotel room, I picked up the journals and read them, first Soc's notes, then my own. When I finally set them down late that night, I had to face the fact that the heart of his message hadn't yet penetrated me. My words had sprung from *his* insight, *his* realization. I'd finally glimpsed the gate he spoke of, but I hadn't yet passed through it. Just before I fell asleep, an odd thought came to me: *Maybe I've already died, and this is the afterlife.*

The shadowy specter followed me down darkened dream streets until I sat up, gasping. My eyes darted around the dark room; I couldn't seem to get enough air. Stumbling to my feet, I splashed cold water over my face and chest at the sink and dressed quickly. Fleeing the confines of my tiny hotel room in the beautiful city of Kyoto, I returned to aimless wandering, desperate to shake off the feeling that I was no longer in the world.

Everywhere I looked, I sensed the fragility of human

life. I had no defense or denial left. In a snap of eternity's finger, I too would fall like the blossoms now strewn in white and pink carpets beneath the cherry trees. The people walking past me would all die too. Even now they appeared as ghostly, transparent figures. No one seemed to take any notice of me, a *gaijin* in a sea of Japanese, increasing my sense of invisibility, my dread of nonbeing.

THIRTY-ONE

I entered a park. All was quiet before the dawn, but inside me a battle raged between love and fear, selfhood and nonbeing. In the first light of dawn, seeking to reestablish my connection to the earth, I did some push-ups, then kicked up to a handstand on a bench. After some stretching, I began the familiar routine of t'ai chi that had become a part of me. Finally my attention settled into the body. *I won't die a victim*, I thought. *Even if I never become a warrior like Socrates, I'll find my own way.*

I returned to my hotel room to get some rest. As soon as I opened the door, I saw him standing there in front of me—with the familiar grin and posture. Socrates hadn't aged at all, at least not in my imagination. It wasn't really him, of course, but an apparition, a reminder that quickly faded. But I could hear his voice saying, "I'm not here for you to trust me, Dan. I'm here to help you trust yourself." I turned to the little samurai on the desk, pointing the way. "Wherever you step," Socrates had written in his letter, "a path will appear."

Leaving the hotel to find my path for the day, for my life, I recalled an uneasy moment during an all-night hike I'd once taken in the woods. With just a sliver of moon showing, my only light was a small headlamp. At one point, about four o'clock in the morning, I realized that I'd lost my way. I slowly backtracked until, ten minutes later, I found the faint outlines of the trail. I felt like that now, the way I had in the moments before my path appeared. I took one step, then another, to see where they might lead.

That day I walked past neighborhood gardens and small Shinto shrines, and I rode several small connector trains to other parts of the city. I let my thoughts roam, trusting my brain to sort through and make sense of all that had transpired.

Disembarking from the local train in the early dusk, I walked through the warm, humid evening back toward my hotel, searching among the small shops for a café where I could find noodles or rice and vegetables. As I passed a magazine stand, the proprietor, an elderly white-haired man, held out an English-language newspaper in both hands for my inspection. After purchasing the paper, I found a nearby eatery where I pointed to a picture of rice, vegetables, and tofu, managing a "*Gohan, yasai, tofu, kudasai*"—reminding the counter clerk that I was a *bejitarian*. I sat down at a plastic table and looked at the newspaper.

On the front page below the fold, a piece caught my eye. It mentioned the eerie woods on the northern base of Mount Fuji that the Japanese called Aokigahara Jukai—the Sea of Trees, or the Suicide Forest. *Isn't that the same place where the aikido master went to die?* I recalled. The article went on to describe it as "a notorious site where so many suicides occur each year, the local government has erected a sign on the main hiking trail urging visitors to think of their families and to contact a suicide prevention group."

My food arrived. I set the newspaper aside. I would finish the article, I decided, on the ride to Aokigahara Jukai.

The next morning I found an English-speaking ticket agent who gave me a schedule and detailed directions. I caught a bus to the northwest side of the Fuji foothills. Then I walked several miles. The article had described how tourists also visited the forest where the bones of long-dead people could be found near more recently deceased bodies. Many of the corpses stayed well hidden, and families seeking the bodies of loved ones might not find them for months, if they found them at all.

When I finally arrived, I entered a thick cover of trees. The air had an odd odor and what I can only describe as a strange energy. I moved deeper into what I already thought of as an underworld, said to be populated by the restless ghosts, demons, and angry spirits associated with those who'd died there. I felt strangely at home.

As I walked farther into the dense woods, the air grew thick, muffled by a blanket of silence. Apparently, birds and other animals avoided the area due to the presence of radon gas, leaving an uncanny, windless stillness. I had found Taishan Forest strange at first, but this place seemed darker, even otherworldly. This time I knew that I couldn't rely on my compass due to the high concentration of volcanic rock and magnetic ore.

I wandered along a marked path, looking for one of the rocky ice caverns or wind tunnels. At the forest's entrance, I'd seen signs posted in multiple languages warning hikers not to leave the trail without twine or tape—"If you don't mark your way back, you could easily be lost!"—and I recalled the diver in the underwater cavern and my own near-death escape at Mountain Springs Summit. *Why tempt the fates?* I thought. *I've pushed my luck far enough for one man.* I'd purchased a roll of twine before entering.

An hour into the forest, I spotted some scattered bones. Human? It was difficult to tell. Since sunlight couldn't break through the dense foliage, there were no distinct shadows. At first I thought that someone was following me, until I recognized the sound I heard as my own footsteps echoing in the dead air. Even with the arrival of late afternoon, the heat and humidity remained oppressive. Several times I ventured off, then followed the twine back to its source and moved off in a different direction.

Other visitors had reported finding decomposing bodies—green and yellow, bloated, covered in mushrooms and other growth, as the corpses fused with nature's organic matter. I found this idea of bodies returning to the earth comforting, and thought again of my friend Chun Han.

Just as I'd started to reel in the twine one last time to return to the trail, I lunged to avoid tripping over a corpse. It appeared to be in the early stages of decomposition, still recognizable as a woman. It gave off a strong odor, sweet and nauseating. I started to look away, to respect its privacy, but something caught my eye. Under the woman's arm I could see the corner of what appeared to be an envelope wrapped in plastic.

Brushing moss off the plastic, I could make out words written in a calligraphic style. Having seen it recently on many signs, I recognized the ideogram for "Kyoto." An address? I pocketed the envelope, then headed back to reach the bus stop before dusk, thinking, *I'll never again be able to visit Chun Han's grave, but maybe I can do a service for this woman.*

When I reached the hotel that night, I stopped at the front desk, pointed to the envelope, and asked what it said. The man at the desk translated: "Please deliver to Kanzaki Roshi, Sanzenji Zen Temple, Nakazashi-ku, Kyoto-shi, Kyoto-fu."

That I could do. I could grant the last wish of this nameless woman.

THIRTY-TWO

After another bus ride and a long walk up a steep grade, I observed the artfully landscaped grounds of the Sanzenji Temple and the backdrop of green mountains in the distance. Smaller than other temples, without any of the tour buses I'd seen parked elsewhere, this temple expressed simplicity, elegance, and solitude—what the Zen monks call *wabi-sabi*. I approached an attendant. "Kanzaki Roshi?" I showed the letter but held it in such a way as to make it clear that I wouldn't relinquish it. Not yet. The attendant gestured to the garden. *Ah, it's going to be a while.*

After the attendant moved away, I explored the garden. Glancing back toward the buildings, I noted the temple's resemblance to a villa. Perhaps it had once been a residence. Deep-purple Japanese maples added contrast to the verdant greenery of moss and pine trees, which had been trimmed to form shapes that radiated serenity and balance.

I knelt by a small pond and watched koi fish glide through clear water. In moments like these, life felt like—what were Mei Bao's words?—"a wonderful dream." *Could I be imagining all of this?* From a certain vantage point, my life seemed to unfold in one visionary experience after another, dreams interspersed with the occasional nightmare, my waking life a suspension between fantastic scenes.

I felt a light touch on one shoulder and turned to see an older man in a monk's robe smiling gently down at me. I rose to my feet and bowed. He spoke in heavily accented English: "I am Kanzaki Roshi. I understand you have a letter for me?"

I introduced myself and, in the Japanese custom, handed him the letter with both hands, then bowed. He took the letter in a similar manner, then opened it. I saw, through the paper, that it was a short letter, one that couldn't have taken more than a few seconds to read. But the *roshi* gazed at the words for more than a minute.

When he looked at me again, I saw that his eyes were moist. "Would you join me for tea?"

"I'd be honored."

A few minutes later, we each knelt at a low table as a kimono-clad woman appeared with the elements of *matcha*, the pungent green tea. She poured steaming water onto the green powder and mixed it rapidly with a whisk. Before taking a sip, I copied the *roshi*'s movements as best I could, turning and admiring the cup, a ritual characteristic of the mindful approach of Zen, bred of long meditation practice.

When we'd finished, the *roshi* asked me how I came to possess the letter and what had led me to deliver it. I explained as simply as I could. When I finished, he bowed again. "Thank you for going to the trouble."

"It was no trouble at all," I said. I wanted to know more, but I didn't want to offend him by asking.

Sensing my question, he said, "Her name was Aka Tohiroshina. She worked part-time here as an attendant. I did my best to counsel and guide her. Not well enough, it seems." He took out the letter and translated it for me.

Respected Kanzaki Roshi,

I'm sorry for taking my life. As you know, it has been a long struggle. I didn't mail this letter in case I changed my mind. I don't expect that it will ever reach you. If by some chance it does, please don't attempt to retrieve my body. I don't wish to cause more troubles. It would be a great service if you could convey my apologies to my mother, who did her best. I thank you for your guidance and care. You made my life more peaceful for a time.

When he finished reading, we rested in silence for a time.

It seemed as if both this young woman and the elder aikido master I'd learned of earlier had succumbed to the demon of depression. I recalled an acquaintance in the San Francisco Bay Area also afflicted with depression, who had, on impulse, leapt from the Golden Gate Bridge, only to become one of the rare few who survived. The fall broke his pelvis and both legs and caused other internal injuries. Several years later, after he'd completely recovered, he revealed that a moment after he committed himself to the air, as he plummeted down for those long seconds, weightless, in a numb and disoriented state of suspension, he changed his mind: he wanted to live. *How many others had also changed their minds on the way down?*

Kanzaki Roshi invited me to walk in the garden with him.

He asked about my presence in Japan, and I explained my interest in practices such as Zen and the martial arts. "I've read enough to understand that the heart of Zen is *zazen* meditation and koan practice leading to direct insight. And I've done a little practice," I told him. He waited for me to continue, so I added, with a smile, "I know too much; I've realized too little."

The *roshi* seemed so receptive that I found myself sharing my deepest thoughts and concerns: "I've done much introspection," I said, "yet my life feels like an unsolved koan. I've been fortunate to have studied with a master whom I call Socrates, after the Greek sage. But I remain restless. . . ." Now I was babbling again. After a pause, I chose my words more carefully, "I hope to gain insight to complement my beginner's understanding."

As we walked, I noticed how the red-and-green maple trees leaned gracefully over the pond and the path of stepping stones surrounded by freshly raked gravel. As nearby gardeners in their two-toed shoes raked the path and trimmed the foliage, the *roshi* said, "Japanese gardeners do not create beauty but merely honor it and cultivate it. Like a wood sculptor who cuts away anything that isn't needed for the final shape, landscape artists remove the extraneous—in the trees and in themselves."

Kanzaki Roshi gestured again toward the moss-covered stones, roots, and water. Pointing to one of the trees, he said, "To the Japanese people, plum is the brave heart, the first tree to blossom after winter's chill." He directed my attention to a small green grove to our right. "Bamboo, with its uprightness, represents honesty." As we walked past the carefully raked area—a sea of sand that held small stone islands and, atop them, small pines pruned in the bonsai style—he added, "We draw inspiration from the pine tree because, steadfast in all seasons, unchanging in shape or color, it evokes strength and constancy."

I told him, "Near the entrance I noticed the branches of a pine tree decorated with many small pieces of white paper, hanging like tiny fruit, with writing on them."

"Prayer messages," he said. "A Shinto tradition."

"But isn't this a Buddhist temple?"

He smiled and shrugged. "Shinto is interwoven into the roots of the earth and of Japanese life. One Shinto belief says that *oni*, bad spirits, gather where dust and dirt accumulate. That's why, for so many Japanese, cleanliness is, as you say, next to godliness. The Shinto religion has ten thousand gods—another way to say that Spirit is everywhere. But students of Zen avoid such abstract ideas, preferring the immediacy of each moment."

"It seems that both Shinto and Zen are so interwoven into Japanese culture that it's difficult for an outsider like me to separate them."

"They do blend somewhat," he said, intertwining the fingers of his two hands. "Yet they are distinct. Shinto, or Way of the Gods, is Japan's indigenous religion and dates back to ancient history. It draws on beliefs in *kami*, or spirit deities of nature, and involves purification rites to atone for wrong deeds and find spiritual balance. Most Japanese practice or honor Shinto in their own way. Zen came more recently to Japan, evolving from the Chinese Buddhism known as Chan, based on the Buddha's Four Noble Truths and Eightfold Path to attain enlightenment and transcend the cycles of life and death and rebirth and suffering. While Buddhism emphasizes study of the sutras and rituals, Zen, as you understand, has a direct approach to enlightenment through the practice of *zazen* and koan work with an experienced teacher to gain insight that may lead to gradual or to sudden enlightenment. While Shinto is traditional and communal, Zen has a simple, individual focus, dependent on the practitioner's own sincere effort and practice.

"In the words of Master Takeda Shingen: 'Zen has no secrets other than seriously thinking about birth-and-death.'"

After my recent experiences, these words struck at the heart of my search.

Perhaps seeing my expression, Kanzaki Roshi smiled and said good-naturedly, "There, Professor Dan, I have used up my allotment of words for the week with this look into the heart of the garden and of Japanese life. Perhaps your own meditation and koan practice can help you to appreciate such concepts directly, beyond the intellect."

I nodded, recalling the young woman's letter that had brought me here. "Recent circumstances have led me to contemplate death more intently. It's been a koanlike preoccupation, which took me to Aokigahara Forest and to your student."

"Soon," he said, "I will perform a ritual that honors her

among those who knew her. She has given us another reminder of impermanence, of how all of us pass through life as in a dream." I felt a chill of recognition as his words captured my present state. *When will I awaken?* I thought.

Abruptly, Kanzaki Roshi turned to me, looked into my eyes, and asked: "What truly brought you to Japan?" His directness surprised me.

I searched for the right words, but none came. So I removed my knapsack and brought out the small samurai, handing it to him with both hands, my head bowed. He accepted it in similar fashion and spoke directly to the statuette: "*So desu!*" he said, a note of intensity in his voice—and something like amazement.

"Sometimes such things happen," he murmured to himself. Then to me: "It seems that you have served another purpose in coming here."

"What purpose?" I asked, curious.

He smiled again, this time the way a child might in anticipation of a surprise. Handing me back the samurai statuette, he said, "I cannot answer you in words. There is another temple, a retreat site. A place so little known, it has no name. With your permission, I'll take you there myself, without delay."

THIRTY-THREE

After a short drive, our car dropped us off at the end of a cul-de-sac. I could see some small homes farther down, but the road ended here, and a thick forest of bamboo began. I followed the *roshi* as he made his way carefully through the bamboo.

Once inside, I found a narrow dirt trail that cut left, then right, before opening onto a wider path paved with stones and gravel. Kanzaki Roshi's robe flapped as he again disappeared at a sharp turn. A few minutes later, I found him waiting for me in a clearing. On the other side of the clearing, near another wall of bamboo, stood what might have been a traditional home, its thick thatch roof steeply pitched, made of what the *roshi* described as rice straw and cedar bark.

The bamboo fence had an entrance, a low gate made of

wooden dowels and woven reeds, which swung upward, forcing would-be entrants to first bend their knees and bow in order to raise the gate, an act of humility, much like the traditional bow of martial arts practitioners as they enter or leave a *dojo*. Kanzaki Roshi moved with grace through the gate and propped it open using a small pole. I followed, also bowing low. He removed the pole, and the gate swung shut behind us. As we approached the house, I saw that its floor was raised slightly off the ground, protection during the rainy season.

We removed our shoes on the small veranda and entered. In the center of the room, a low table squatted over a small fire pit, which would serve both cooking and heating purposes. Older but immaculate tatami mats covered the floor. A single window let in a soft light. The walls were made of rice paper panels.

We passed quickly through this room. Kanzaki Roshi slid open a panel leading to a covered walkway with a view of another pristine garden, smaller than the temple's. Along the length of the walkway, closed panels led to other rooms, which, once opened, would look directly out into the garden. Now the *roshi* slipped his feet into sandals and bid me do the same. Radiating the same childlike enthusiasm he'd shown before, he led me to a far corner of the garden and onward along a winding path of irregular stones, ending at a waist-high boulder, its top flattened.

On the boulder's surface stood two small samurai statuettes nearly identical to mine in age and appearance, facing away from each other at an angle. Each warrior stood in a different posture: The first, the *roshi* explained, stood in the classic water stance, with the sword held in front of the body, hands and hilt near the waist, sword tip pointing upward toward an invisible adversary's throat. The second warrior stood in the fire stance, with the sword held high, the hands over the forehead, and the sword tip pointing back and up, ready to strike downward in an instant. Both classic fighting postures.

The *roshi* pointed to a slightly discolored oval where a third statue must have stood. He turned to me and waited. I drew out my own samurai and set it in the third place, turning it one way, then another. Only when I turned its back to the other two did it fit perfectly into the slight hollow of the boulder. Now the three samurai stood in a triangle, each facing out, alert, each guarding the others' backs. I'd considered my little samurai's posture many times without any idea of what it meant. Unlike the other two swordsmen, his blade remained in its scabbard (or *saya*), his hand on the hilt—not a fighting posture, but ready—a peaceful warrior.

For a few moments, I may have stopped breathing. *How can this be?* I wondered. Memories unspooled in my mind: finding the little samurai many months before in an underwater cave; carrying it with me through the desert; letting it point me onward to the city of Hong Kong, then to Taishan Forest and the school, and finally here. The little samurai had found his way home. I had no answer, but there was a rightness to it.

The triad was now complete—and so, it seemed, was my journey. What had begun as a mystery ended in one. For a few more moments, I gazed in at this mysterious reunion. Then, with a bow to the three samurai, I let it go, and the revelation passed like a sunburst or a rain shower. I think Socrates would have been pleased.

As the *roshi* and I walked away, words from the journal came to mind: "*memory, what you call the past, and imagination, what you call the future. . . .*"

As we removed our garden shoes on reaching the walkway, Kanzaki Roshi moved ahead and slid open a panel to one of the rooms facing the garden. "Before you go, perhaps you might find some benefit in sitting *zazen* for a time?"

"I'd like that," I said.

"Begin with half an hour—you'll hear a gong. After sitting, you can practice *kinhin*, walking meditation, until your legs feel limber and you're ready to sit once again. Increase the time of each sitting practice through the night."

I have nowhere else to be here or now, I thought, grateful for the opportunity.

Before he left me, I asked, "Do you have any other words of advice about how I might meditate properly?"

"Just two things," he answered. "You need good posture. And you need to die." He turned and departed silently from the room, closing the panel behind him.

I'd like to say that my mind emptied of all thought, but his departing words had the opposite effect.

How do I die? I brooded. *Is this what he means by good posture? Maybe he hasn't left yet. . . .* I shook off the impulse to open my eyes, to look up, to give up.

I imagined monks sitting somewhere not far away, in absolute stillness, with nothing above their shoulders but the sky, experiencing no-mind, or *mushin*, as Kanzaki Roshi had called it. Meanwhile, a veritable Disneyland operated inside my skull. I did my best not to move or fidget, even when my nose itched. Even when I had to sneeze. *No!* I thought. *You must not sneeze! No sneeze, no sneeze, no sneeze,* I repeated as the urge grew. I started to sweat with the effort of all these shoulds. *Posture . . . die—what does it all mean anyway? I'm such a mess! If Socrates could see the state of my mind—why did he ever take me on as his student?*

In-breath and out-breath, reception and release. Inspiration, inhaling spirit. Expiration, letting go. Again and again I turned my attention back to the breath, only the breath. . . .

In this manner I sat for longer periods; in needed interludes, I stood and performed a slow, conscious walking meditation, attending to the shift of weight as one foot after the other moved forward, filling and emptying, in the manner of t'ai chi. After completing a circuit of the room, with my eyes still half-lidded, I sat again.

Just after dawn, a gong sounded six times. I slowly lifted my half-closed eyes from the tatami mat. I can't really explain what happened next, but when I opened my eyes fully, I blinked, then blinked again, unable to grasp the familiar form in front of me.

"*Socrates?*" I said.

He sat there grinning, just as he had grinned in the hotel room. He reached up, scratched his face, and slid open a panel, letting in the light.

THIRTY-FOUR

As I looked on, Socrates knelt in the Japanese style. Wearing the black *hakama* pants and white cotton *uwagi* jacket, he appeared older, venerable, ethereal. Yet his eyes still held their sparkle. The time we'd spent together came rushing back; the years since compressed into what seemed like no time at all.

"Hi, junior," he said. "Late, as usual. Any stories you'd like to share?"

I didn't need an invitation. I told him of my life since we were last together—about my failing marriage and how much I missed my daughter. About my time with Mama Chia in the rain forest, and how I'd found the samurai statue and his letter and, later, the journal. I described Ama and Papa Joe, who had helped him all those years ago, and the boy who became Joe Stalking Wolf, and my travels to Hong Kong and China, and about Hua Chi and Mei Bao and Master Ch'an and Chun Han and my students.

I began to tell him more about the journal that Nada—María—had committed to his care. As I moved to get it, he stilled me.

"No need. Please continue."

So I described what had happened since my arrival in Japan, including my journey through the Aokigahara Jukai, which had led me to Kanzaki Roshi and to the present moment.

I asked for his guidance. "I can't shake a feeling of unreality, Soc—as if I'm caught in a dream, looking over a precipice, haunted again by that dark specter of death."

He said nothing in response, but continued to gaze at me. Until, finally, he said only this: "We may meet again, when you're ready."

"I get that a lot," I said testily. "Ready for what?"

"For death. For life. For whatever may come."

"We're meeting right now, Soc. Isn't now your favorite time?"

In the silence that followed, it felt as if we'd never parted, which was in some sense true. But he had changed somehow. Or maybe it was me.

When I looked up, Soc's body suddenly began to shimmer and then changed into the hooded specter of death. In shock, I closed my eyes to shut out the vision. When I opened them again, it was Kanzaki Roshi who sat serenely in front of me, wearing the identical clothing that Socrates had worn. Stunned, I stammered, "How—how long have you been sitting there? Have we been speaking?"

"You spoke. I sat."

"But he told me things—he was here. . . ."

The *roshi* rose to his feet. "Please, Dan-san, continue your practice."

Clambering to my feet, I staggered down the hall to relieve myself. I found cold water in a pitcher just outside the room and drank, feeling even more rattled than I had the night before.

When I returned to *zazen*, I struggled to find a relaxed, upright posture, "neither leaning forward into the future nor backward into the past," as Socrates had once told me. Socrates. I was so sure he'd been here, moments before. *I wish I'd told him about the writing. Even if his appearance was some kind of illusion.*

An illusion—like the self, like death, I thought—returning to what Kanzaki Roshi had said. *Why must I die in order to meditate properly?*

Out of the stillness, an answer appeared: While alive, I remain attached to the business of the world, engaged on a moving walkway of passing plans, questions, and thoughts.

For the dead, no attachments remain. There's nothing left to do, to accomplish, to grasp.

I recalled the yoga practice of *shavasana*, the corpse pose, to complete *asana* practice. It was meant to be more than a relaxation exercise. *But what does it mean to let go of all that is life? What must I relinquish in order to die?* Such questions had become seeds that, when planted deep within, began to grow and bear fruit. Soon I fell into a spontaneous meditation. Unlike the usual sitting practice, this was filled with revelation. It came in a flood that took form only when I later wrote it all down.

It begins by exhaling darkness and inhaling light, until my physical form fills with a sparkling blue-white light. . . .

Next comes a profound willingness to surrender, returning to what I was before I was conceived, to die while I live, to let go completely, to relinquish everything and enter the experience and process of dying, starting with . . .

No more time. Past and future vanish as I surrender all memory and imagination. Only the present remains.

No more objects. All possessions vanish: toys, tools, keepsakes, clothing. All I own, all I've earned, collected, or purchased. I will leave the world as I arrived. Naked.

No more relations. I bid farewell to every human and animal I know or have ever known: family, friends, colleagues, acquaintances, childhood pets. . . . All those I love, and who love me, vanish. From this point I'm alone.

No more action. I release the ability to move, to speak, to do, to influence, to accomplish . . . no more duties or responsibilities . . . no task to complete or business to finish as my body turns as immobile as wood.

No more emotion. The colors of feeling fade into gray . . . no joy or sorrow, fear or courage, anger or serenity, passion, melancholy or elation, as the heart and whole body turn to stone.

Now the senses depart, one by one:

No more savoring. The power of taste vanishes . . . no more food, drink, or lover's lips to stimulate tongue or palate with sweetness or spice.

No more smell. The end of all scents and fragrances . . . of food and flowers . . . gone are aromas of those I love, of home and hearth, of the natural world.

No more sight. Images lose focus, then there's nothing more to focus upon . . . the beauty of nature's landscapes, the colors of sunrise or sunset, the sensual shapes of the world, the colors and textures, the light and shadow—all fade into darkness.

No more sound. The capacity to hear music and voices, the songs of birds, a rustle of leaves or silk, wind chimes, laughter, and thunder, the sounds of city life—all slip into silence, even the thrum of my blood while it still flows in my veins.

No more sensation. The end of pain or pleasure,

warmth or cold . . . never again feeling the skin-to-skin touch of a loved one as nerve endings grow numb.

Without time, objects, relations, actions, emotions, or the senses of taste, smell, sight, hearing, or touch, only darkness and silence remain.

No more self. No sense of being or having a body . . . the last remaining thread or experience of an inner self is cut. . . . Finding the center of the paradox, letting go of what never truly existed. Fading, growing transparent, weightless, vanishing. Only Consciousness remains. And the world goes on exactly as it was, without me.

THIRTY-FIVE

The sound of a gong brought me back to myself in a silent room. It took a few moments for me to realize where I was, who I was. Having relinquished all the experiences, relations, sensations, and memories that comprised my life, I might have expected a bittersweet sense of sorrow. Instead, I felt reborn. Because, when I opened my eyes, the gifts of life all came flooding back.

I had a past to remember and a future to imagine! I could enjoy objects and possessions without being as attached to them. I had loved ones, friends, colleagues, and innumerable acquaintances to enjoy. I could deeply feel emotions changing like the weather, like the seasons. I could savor the delights of food and drink, smell aromas, see a world of light and color, hear a symphony of sounds, and interact with people and the world around me through the gift of touch. *This is what it means to be alive.*

As I sat in the quiet room, I recalled a story Socrates had told me about a great turtle who swam through the depths of the seven seas, surfacing for a single breath only once every hundred years. "Imagine a wooden ring," he said, "drifting on the surface of one of the vast oceans. What are the odds that this turtle would surface and just happen to stick his head up through the center of that wooden ring?"

"One in a trillion, I suppose—close to zero chance."

"Consider how the odds of being born a human being on planet Earth are less than that."

And what are the odds, I thought, *that I'm here now, in a Zen temple in Kyoto, Japan, on planet Earth, playing the odd role of Dan Millman in a limited engagement?*

That evening, Kanzaki Roshi and I shared a quiet meal before he took his leave, inviting me to spend one more evening in the temple of the three samurai.

Just before sleep that night, I packed Soc's journal and my notebook back into my knapsack, folded my clothes for the journey home. And, thinking about my daughter, I carefully tucked in the kachina doll.

In the morning, after a light breakfast, I found a car waiting to take me back to Osaka and the airport.

As the jet passed through the evening sky, flashes of lightning lit the clouds below, and I floated once again between heaven and earth, on the way home.

EPILOGUE

Before I landed in Ohio and returned to my daughter, my classes, and the conventions of everyday life, I heard Soc's voice as clearly as if he were sitting in the empty seat beside me. I could almost see him out of the corner of my eye and feel his hand on my shoulder as his voice rang out in my mind: "You expected to find a hidden school in the East, Dan, so that's where I sent you. But now you understand that the hidden school appears in every forest, park, city, or town, whenever you look beyond the surface of things. You need only wake up and open your eyes."

Socrates had sent me to find a hidden school somewhere so that I might discover it everywhere, and finally realize that the promise of eternal life awaits us all—not on the other side of death, but here and now, in the eternal present.

My report to the dean and grant committee was well received. In the months that followed, I shared a few insights from the journal with those friends and colleagues who were interested, keeping in mind the wisdom of the Indian sage Sai Baba of Shirdi, who once said, "I give people what they want so that eventually they may want what I want to give them."

That December, at the end of the term, I withdrew from my faculty position. My wife and daughter and I moved back to Northern California. Once they were settled into their own place, I found a small apartment not far away and lived in solitude.

Months passed. Winter turned to spring. Then, one summer evening, I opened my wallet and drew out Soc's business card. The faded words printed on the front—*Paradox, Humor, Change*—now held new meaning and depth. I turned the card over. To my surprise, I found four words written there, and a set of numbers. Mystified, I read: "Edison Lake, south side." I'd once visited that area on a backpacking trip east of Merced in the Sierra National Forest.

Is it Soc's handwriting or my own? I wondered. Could I have walked in my sleep, opened the wallet, and written those words? Was the message connected to my real or imagined meeting with Socrates during my final days in Japan?

I studied the numbers: 8–27–76. August twenty-seventh, four days from now. One way or the other, I sensed, it would be the end of a long journey. Or was it my flight to Samarra? Would the dark specter be waiting for me, or a vision of eternal life? I heard Soc's voice ring out in my mind: "Consciousness is not *in* the body, Dan; the body is in Consciousness. And *you* are that Consciousness. . . . When you relax mindless into the body, you're happy and content and free. . . . Immortality is *already* yours."

That night, somewhere in the labyrinthine dream world, a gap opened in the lining of time and space. What emerged was a vision of my future, a bare possibility:

My body begins to tremble, and I fall backward through space. Thousands of feet above a patchwork of green and brown far below, my arms stretch out to the horizon. Held aloft by the wind. Once again I'm a point of awareness floating on a cushion of air between heaven and earth. A forest appears below, growing closer as distinct shapes come into focus—a barn and fields and a stream running past a white pavilion. I yearn to soar upward again, away from a world of gravity and mortality. But I fall from the sky, down toward a beach where white sand meets blue sea. As I spin downward, whirling now, the wind becomes a roar, then absolute silence, as I pass through the earth and soar upward again and into the night as shining orbs congeal into a tunnel of light. . . .

The light becomes a crackling campfire illuminating the face of my old mentor as he sits in a forest clearing. He's been waiting for me all along. His eyes shine. Bright sparks float up into the night sky until the firelight turns to starlight.

ACKNOWLEDGMENTS

No one writes a high-quality book on their own. Without the support of my literary agent, Stephen Hanselman; my publisher, Michele Martin; my enthusiastic senior editor, Diana Ventimiglia; my copy editor, Joal Hetherington; Cindy Ratzlaff, Jean Anne Rose, and the entire team at Simon & Schuster's North Star Way imprint—as well as early readers Ned Leavitt, Alyssa Factor, David Cairns, Holly Deme, Peter Ingraham, Ed St. Martin, Dave Meredith, David Moyer, and Martin Adams—this book would not exist in its present form.

Special thanks to my wife, Joy, who read multiple rough drafts and provided invaluable guidance as the manuscript took shape, and to our daughter, author Sierra Prasada, whose in-depth developmental guidance and line editing made possible a more coherent narrative. My longtime freelance editor, Nancy G. Carleton, provided a final polish.

Appreciation to the following individuals for their insight, information, and suggestions: Reb Anderson Roshi, Linda Badge, Clark Bugbee, Mickey Chaplan, Annie Liou, Takashi Shima, and Harumi Yamanaka. Author and t'ai chi teacher Scott Meredith shared expertise related to the internal-energy aspects and history of t'ai chi.

As always, love and gratitude to my late parents, Herman and Vivian Millman, who continue to inspire me with their example and memory.

The following books served as background insight and inspiration: *Knocking on Heaven's Door* by Katy Butler; *How We Die* by Sherwin Nuland, MD; *The Final Crossing* by Scott Eberle; *Autumn Lightning* by Dave Lowry; *The Professor in the Cage* and *The Storytelling Animal* by Jonathan Gottschal; *Zen and Japanese Culture* and *Zen and the Samurai* by D. T. Suzuki; *From Here to Here* by Gary Crowley; *Free Will* by Sam Harris; *Being Mortal* by Atul Gawande; *Do No Harm* by Henry Marsh; *The Self Illusion* by Bruce Hood; *When Breath Becomes Air* by Paul Kalanithi; *Life and Death in Shanghai* by Nien Cheng; *Smoke Gets in Your Eyes* by Caitlin Doughty; *The Way of Zen* by Alan Watts; *How to Sit* by Thich Nhat Hanh; *On Death and Dying* by Elisabeth Kübler-Ross; and *The Death of Ivan Ilyich* by Leo Tolstoy.